DEDICATION

I first dedicate this book to my loving and committed wife who stands with me as we fulfill God's purpose in life.

I also dedicate this book to Pastor John Hagee who has taught me the discipline and passion expressed in this directive for the last 40 years: "Do it everytime like it's your last time, because one day it will be."

I also dedicate this book to my father who encouraged me to seek God's will and my mother who taught me to sing and to maximize my potential.

And I also express my appreciation to Ron Acosta and Tommy and Christi Moorman for their support in making this book possible.

Contents

Introduction	6
Section I — The Foundation to Health, Life, and Happiness	
Chapter #1: The Foundation to Freedom	15
Chapter #2: Learned Behavior	29
Section II — The Laws that Govern You	
Chapter #3: The Law of the Mind	49
Chapter #4: The Law of Action	62
Section III — Dealing with Your Past	
Chapter #5: Resolving Your Past	81
Chapter #6: A Real Story of Resolving the Past	99
Testimony: Terri's Story	99
Chapter #7: Practical Next Steps	114
Section IV — Restoring Your Health	
Chapter #8: Applying Love to Your Self-Image	129
Chapter #9: Do You Want Your Health Back?	139
Chapter #10: Trauma Bonding and Relationships	149
Chapter #11: Overcoming Fears	157
Section V — Setting Your Mind in Order	
Chapter #12: Retraining Your Mind	167

Chapter #13: Steps Required for Lasting Change   178
Chapter #14: Target Your Thoughts to Take Control   187
Chapter #15: Put Emotions in Their Place   200

Section VI — Steps to Maximizing Your Potential
Chapter #16: Maximizing Your Potential   212
Chapter #17: Envision Your Future   218
   Testimony: A True Story   224

Summary   229

Introduction

Have you ever wondered:

- Why do I negatively respond the way I do?
- Why are my emotions so oversensitive?
- Why do my emotions rule over me with such overwhelming power?
- Why do my negative emotions go so deep and stay there so long?

Or maybe you've thought to yourself:

- Why do I take things so personally?
- Why do I struggle with such fear, anger, and rejection?
- Why do I get so depressed and feel like a dark cloud is hanging over my head?
- Why do I feel so uncomfortable when in a close and intimate setting or in front of crowds?
- Why do I feel so empty and unfulfilled?

Or maybe in a quiet moment you asked yourself:

- Why am I so angry?

- Why am I tormented with thoughts, emotions, and feelings?
- Why can't I stop addictive patterns?
- Why can't I feel better about myself?
- Why can't I be attracted to someone who is good for me rather than to relationships that hurt me?

If any of the questions hit home, then you are among the walking wounded. A wound is created by any negative experience that causes emotional pain in you. These pains can be caused by rejection, abandonment, neglect, abuse, not being loved, etc., that come from experiences such as divorce, abuse (sexual, physical, verbal), death, abortions, separation, etc. As a result of wounds, you can develop a "wound behavior." A wound behavior is a behavior that you learn and practice during the time that you are wounded and you typically practice those behaviors potentially far beyond the time that you are well.

Of course it is possible that you never got well and you stayed wounded. Regardless, these wounds and the behaviors they caused must be recognized and dealt with in order to be really resolved. In fact, you can even be healed from your wounds and still act out wound behaviors. The best case scenario is to heal the wound and dismantle the wound behavior so that you act healed instead of acting wounded.

A wound is created by any negative experience that hurt, violated, or traumatized you, all of which produced pain in your life. Some experiences are more painful and impacting than others.

Wounds can be self-inflicted or inflicted by someone or something else. The pain usually creates a negative "reference point" in the emotions, mind, body, self-esteem, and memories.

Some wounds impact the emotions to such an extent that it creates ongoing stress. If this stress is at a high level and recurring, it can develop into a stress or anxiety disorder. Sometimes these disorders develop during the wounding because the wound is so severe and traumatizing. Stress disorders come in the following forms: Post

Traumatic Stress Disorder, Acute Stress Disorder, and Chronic Stress Disorder. Anxiety Disorders can develop into Generalized Anxiety or Panic Disorder.

A wound can be from the recent or distant past, but if it remains unaddressed and unhealed, it will remain unresolved. An unresolved wound will push outward into your behavior. These wound behaviors will not heal over time because time alone does not heal a wound. Time allows you to address or ignore the wound. Time will give more opportunity for you to deal with it or ignore it, but it will not go away on its own.

You cannot control a wound or suppress it forever. Eventually you will not be strong enough to suppress or control the wound and the hypersensitivities that are associated with it. It will eventually push outward into your behavior and be revealed in your behavior. You may try to avoid or deny the wound behaviors, but you cannot hide them forever.

> **You cannot control a wound or suppress it forever.**

Trying to hide them will create a fear that other people will detect your behaviors and that fear will eventually torment you and make you oversensitive or hypersensitive to certain topics related to the fear. The fear can even help you misinterpret what others say and believe the fear messages and feelings inside of you rather than your rational mind and facts. This kind of fear will convince you that your fears are the facts, and that the fear messages are valid and telling the truth.

Why wounds are seldom fixed

A wound behavior may not be immediately recognized as being related to a wound because it hides behind justifications. This is why the wound often remains unresolved. You may not connect the dots between a negative recurring pattern in your behavior and the wound from which it originated. If you do connect those dots and recognize the association, the justifications you feel or make each time you act on the negative behaviors seem to enable it and keep it in place as a justified and legitimate behavior.

You should recognize your negative behavior patterns (behavior that reoccurs) and rather than automatically validate them, decide to stop them and replace them with new positive ones. If you are consistently (not necessarily "constantly") acting or reacting in ways that are unwanted, negative, or destructive, then you must examine your life and ask yourself the question why?

Behavior is not accidental. Wounds are a part of life and to believe that you have not been wounded is a delusion, denial, ignorance, fear, avoidance, or maybe just not knowing how to change it, but you know that at times something is wrong in your thinking, emotions, and responses. If you know you overreact and you do it too often, do not just push it aside as imperfection. It is a wound behavior.

A wound behavior is a behavior that develops and is learned during the time that you are wounded. If, for example, you broke your leg, then you would compensate for the pain, weakness, trauma, and cast by limping, walking slower, being overly cautious, using a crutch, keeping people at a distance, using medication, etc. Then after the leg is healed, you would practice these wound behaviors because you learned them during the time of the wound.

The same is true with emotional wounds. If those emotional wounds are not healed, the wound behaviors will continue until the wound is identified, forgiven (God, self, others), and confessed.

Even if the wound is healed, a wound behavior can continue!

WHAT ABOUT YOU?

It is important for you to examine your life right now and ask yourself if you have unresolved wounds or are suffering from wound behaviors.

You can identify a wound behavior by looking at yourself to see if you frequently react to small offenses with high intensity over a long period of time. If so, this is a sign of a wound behavior!

The way you identify the wound behind the reaction is the "theme" of the topic you overreact to and the hypersensitivity in you regarding certain topics. Examples include recurring feelings of rejection, failure, not being important, not being valued, abandonment, betrayal, etc.

If you look back, you can examine all of your reactions and familiar feelings that you have had to overcome, fight, and push away. These wound themes show up in the form of fear, and recurring fears about the same topics or themes are signs of wound behaviors.

If you are tired of the same old personal struggles and you really desire to be free, then this book is for you. I believe this book is God-inspired and will provide you with profound revelations and insights for which you have been searching.

The following partial list of human problems represents internal wounds that are often hidden inside of us and influence our thinking, conduct, emotions, feelings, decisions, and behavior. Which of these strike a nerve within you:

- Fear and fear-based control mechanisms
- Self-defense mechanisms
- Lack of intimacy
- Insecurities
- Inferiorities
- Phobias
- Paranoia's
- Being overly sensitive
- Torment
- Recurring personal offenses
- Continued grudges
- Betrayal
- Anxiety
- Panic

- Stress disorders
- Depression (situational or clinical)
- Eating disorders
- Social fears
- Rage
- Addictions (drug, alcohol, sexual, pornography, spending)
- Self-mutilation (cutting, burning, etc.)
- Obesity
- Hoarding
- Isolation
- Detaching
- Hopelessness
- Suicide

Also included in this list are recurring self-perceptions and feelings of being unimportant, not loved, not valued, left out, not included, a failure, weak, unstable, inadequate, not good enough, used, abandoned, not accepted, not approved of, rejected, not wanted, unworthy, not deserving of good, cursed, invalid, incapable, confused, underdeveloped, not recognized, and not appreciated.

There is no shame in reaching out for help.

Do these words seem familiar to you? Have they re-visited you throughout your life? Are they the same internal messages and feelings that influence you too often? Are you tired of repeating these same patterns of thoughts, feelings, and behavior? In this book, I will provide you with the answers to these questions and more.

It is time to be free!

There is a way for you to not only get free, but to actually stay free from these troubling and all too familiar issues. If you think you already know the answers to your problems and you don't need any help, you should realize that no one person has all the answers. What's more, if you did, you would have solved them by now.

There is no shame in reaching out for help so that you can experience healing. There is, on the other hand, shame in having the opportunity to be helped and refusing it. I encourage you to open your mind and your heart and prepare yourself to receive the truths and revelations you will find in this book.

If you are ready for help, then it is time to resolve your past, restore your health, and retrain your thinking.

Let's begin!

Walking Wounded is a book that explains how people get wounded and how they never really purposefully resolve those wounds. As a result, they act out "wounded behaviors" created from those wounds.

To resolve and heal wounds, they must be identified and dealt with intentionally, otherwise they will remain active, but suppressed, until the next time they are triggered.

Walking Wounded teaches you how to experience wholeness (spirit, soul, and body) and maximize your God-given potential in life!

Section I

The Foundation to Health, Life, and Happiness

The Foundation of health, life, and happiness is found in resolving your past, restoring your health (spirit, mind, emotions, and body), retraining your mind, removing distractions (fears, bad relationships, and busywork), identifying your personal gifting and personality strengths, and maximizing that potential inside of you. This does not mean you have to be perfect or mistake-free. The fact is that you will never satisfy perfectionist demands.

Rather, you can develop and maximize on your God-given giftings, personality strengths and talents that will fulfill you and always work for you and always bring you happiness. Last, but not least, you must recognize your need for God in your life. The time will always come when you will not be powerful and adequate enough to solve all your problems, crises, and wounds in life. You need God's help and love to get you through.

Without His empowerment, you will experience death of many kinds. With Him you will experience life.

CHAPTER 1

THE FOUNDATION TO FREEDOM

The fact is, tangible problems rarely do as much damage as the behaviors that people practice in response to life's problems. Many people experience internal prolonged suffering that is mostly self-induced. It is the result of something in their past that is still affecting their ability to respond and problem solve correctly.

If the past remains unresolved, it will keep you in an emotional prison that will rule you until you finally deal with it and get it resolved. Everyone has wounds, traumas, sins and mistakes in their past. There are no exceptions! The only question is whether or not you are aware that the wounds are still negatively influencing you.

It is time to change. You cannot continue to act like everything is okay when it is not. You cannot hide the wounds and the wound behaviors associated with them. They will come out eventually and they will be seen.

Attempts to hide the wound behaviors will require that you develop a secret world of behavior that is not seen by others. These kinds of secret identities will keep you constantly wondering if the wounds and their behaviors will be detected. Then you will have to deny they are there or lash out to keep people away. You may also revert to avoidance, isolation, or blame in order to cover them up. You must realize that covering them up will protect them and keep them in place inside of you. Consequently they will become stronger and more automatic in you, and therefore harder to break.

The truth is, secrecy cannot protect you. Every wound will eventually become apparent. There is nothing hidden that will not be revealed in some way.

You have wasted too much of your life and precious time avoiding or trying to solve these problems by yourself. Once and for all, it is time to be free. It is time to experience long-lasting change.

I may not have listed your exact problem, but do not use that as an excuse to avoid any more. Even if you are afraid of dealing with these issues, the fear that you obey will not deliver or heal you from your unhealthy, tormented, or deficient existence. The fear cannot and does not protect you. Stuffing problems hurts, and angers won't help either. Eventually they will come up and negatively influence your life, and most likely already have. It is time to change and it is time to be healthy.

GETTING HEALTHY IS THE GOAL

"Health" is the definition of "success," according to Americans surveyed in a Gallup poll conducted a few years ago. Health includes elements that are spiritual, mental, emotional, physical, relational, economical, professional, self-image, etc. People are unhealthy, that's a given, and some of those people are willing to change and others are unwilling to change. Which are you?

> **You are waiting on a crisis to force you to make changes.**

I believe that God Himself desires for you to be healthy in every way possible. Success, health, and change are not just for someone else. It is for you and it is your time now. It is for all those who are willing or desperate enough to step out and act, even at the expense of fear and the risk of failure.

I can tell you that every time I have accomplished something that I previously thought to be too difficult, I have always looked back and wondered why I did not do it sooner. It always had something to do with some kind of fear.

No matter what has happened to you in life, whether self-inflicted or not, failure is not permanent unless you decide it is by escaping or quitting. Quitting is not the same as recovering. You should and must recover from wounds. *Failure is not just an experience, but more so, it is an attitude and a decision, and possibly a spiritual problem as well.*

In the midst of failure, be encouraged to know that you possess God-given gifts inside of you on a spirit level that never go away, regardless. You can always access them. In fact they are the automatic strengths, passion, and positives that flow through you. A gift is an endowment that you can develop and maximize but that you did not earn. It was there at birth and is still ready to be maximized. No matter at what level you function in life, your gifts make you unique and they make room for you.

Many people make resolutions for the New Year or at other times during their life, usually because they realize they need to change. These resolutions often represent the recognition of problems or personal, recurring negative patterns. Resolutions are broken and fade away, but the problem does not disappear.

The definition of resolution is: "fixed purpose in determination of mind ... as a resolution to reform our lives ... a resolution to undertake an expedition ... constancy in execution, implying courage."

You may not realize it, but what you are waiting on is a crisis to force you to make changes. You will not change or improve merely because you need to change. You will change when you desire to have something better or desire to get away from the pain and suffering you feel.

Nevertheless, you must have desperation along with that desire to go beyond the crisis and pain, for it must not be your only motivator. If you are crisis motivated, then you will most likely fall back into your old patterns after the crisis is over. If you do improve, it will be a slight change that really does not have much measurable difference in the fruit you bear in life.

SIGNS OF REAL CHANGE

In the final analysis, results are the only accurate measuring tool. Sincerity, tears, or crisis are often used to measure change. They are not dependable measuring tools because of the normal tendencies in people to be motivated into action during the crisis and let up when they feel better.

Many clients through the years come into my office in a desperate condition, either in their relationships or with personal problems. I warn them that even though they will feel better from the therapy, they must push through until their issues are resolved, and they must replace the old patterns with new ones. But they don't realize that they are crisis motivated, which means when they are no longer in a crisis (situationally or emotionally), they stop working on themselves because they feel better. However, they end up getting back into their old condition or even worse, because they didn't finish the treatment and do the necessary work. Others do this because they try to control everything, even deciding that they don't need help anymore, just because they got some information that relieved them, but will not permanently change them. It is like starting an antibiotic for an infection and discontinuing it half way through because you feel better. You feel better, but the healing process is not complete.

I am often asked as a counselor, "How do I know they will change this time?"

My universal answer for everyone is the same and that is, "You will know them by the fruit," and fruit is your consistent behavior acted out after the crisis or pain has ended.

Behavior is not accidental. It is created by thought processes (secret or open) that are practiced over time. By the time the behavior is obvious, it is a result of an internal process that has occurred over time. This is why you can have confidence in measuring behavior.

This does not mean that you judge or condemn people. You can walk into a garden and observe the fruit in that garden or orchard and measure that quality and existence of fruit and tell whether it is good or bad, or if any fruit is there at all. The fruit speaks for itself.

The condition you are in right now is a result of the way you think and believe. There are consequences to choices. God still loves you, but He allows you to maintain the authority and power to choose. You will not be perfect in everything you choose, but you can make quality choices that obviously bless your life instead of curse it. Usually bad choices are made because people do not listen to wise counsel and instruction, but rather choose to learn by pain and suffering. This is called "doing it the hard way." You do not have to do it the hard way, but if you are determined to do so, God will allow it. There is an easier and more effective way and that is to:

- Learn by instruction.
- Stay out of rebellion.
- If you are wounded, do everything you can to heal and maximize your potential (your ability and capacity to develop and use personal gifts, talents, and personality strengths) in life.

When you do this, you will be fulfilled and live a purpose-filled life.

How counseling began for me

I became licensed with the State of Texas as a Marriage and Family Therapist in 1992. Before then, I conducted what is now known as "faith based" counseling. I have done this as an ordained minister since 1986.

Somehow, I often would know the answers to problems that people presented to me. The answers would just come into my mind and I would communicate the logic, direction, and insight that provided answers to people's questions and solutions to their problems.

During that time, I realized that the "ability" to give solutions and insight to people's problems was a God-given gift that was operating in me. I knew it wasn't just my natural abilities because at that time I was just working on my Associates degree in Sociology, and the problems in people's lives were too complex for my natural mind and training to comprehend and solve. My God-given gifts already inside of me were enabling me beyond my natural abilities. This excited me and made me realize that I should become more purposeful and passionate about developing my gifts.

As a counselor, I have had years of intense therapy sessions. Many of these sessions have been life-changing experiences for my clients and for me as well. As a result of these experiences, I have developed a divinely-inspired program called the Trinity Program.

THE TRINITY PROGRAM: RESOLVE, RESTORE, RETRAIN®

I believe God gave me the concept out of a realization that clients needed to experience a level of inner healing that they could not receive from one-on-one therapy sessions alone. When you have Trinity, you have a tri-union of power and purpose to transform people from one place in their inner being to another.

My program is designed to transition you from one state of being to another so that you can resolve your past, remove distractions, maximize your potential, and fulfill your purpose.

> You can never be totally free ... until your wounds are healed.

The Trinity Program represents the three-fold purpose in everything that I do:

Part #1 — Resolve your Past

We have already determined that you must resolve your wounded past or it will preoccupy you, torment you, shame you, keep you in bondage, and push forward into your present behavior. It will do so in the form of some overcompensation or hypersensitivity (i.e. anxiety, anger, depression, seclusion, etc.) that we listed earlier.

You can never be totally free until you identify all of your past hurts and wounds, confess them, heal them, process out of them correctly, and replace them with healthy thinking and behaviors. When your past is confessed and forgiven, then a healing will take place that is an inner healing.

The first phase of the Trinity Program is confession and inner healing. This will set you up for restoration.

Part #2 — Restore your Health

When you were born, your self-worth and image were innocent and moldable. Self-worth is the way you value yourself and it creates perceptions about how others value you. Self-image is how you see yourself (the image you have of yourself). It is also the reflection of what is on the inside of you projected out and how you perceive other's image of you.

A child's primary self-worth is developed during ages 0-12 and the self-image from ages 12-20 (approximately, depending on personality type and developmental factors). During these developmental years, a child's interaction with his/her caretakers and their interfacing with the child will mold the child's worth and image. The caretakers can be biological parents or other people who take on this role.

I believe that God originally intended for those caretakers to be the parents. However, because of life circumstances, other loving family members or friends step in and raise children (and I say God bless them for taking on that awesome responsibility). The health of the caretakers and the way they interact with and train the child will

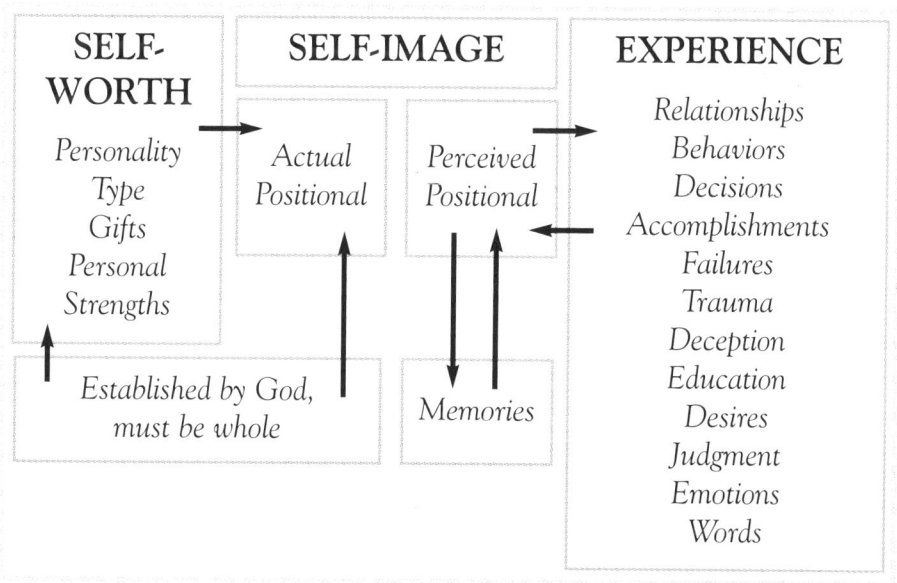

mold that child's self-worth and image and determine how much value the child places on himself/herself.

I believe parents/caretakers should train children to:

- Base their self-worth in God.
- Believe they are valuable because they exist in this world.
- Believe they are valuable because they exist for eternity.
- Believe they are valuable because they have a God-given purpose to fulfill.

On the contrary, many parents train their children to have low self-worth and not to esteem themselves. This is evident by the way the parents abuse or show spiritual, mental, emotional, and physical neglect.

In the Trinity Program, attendees learn that they are valuable, God loves them, and they can restore and reconstruct by design their self-worth and self-image, so they can healthily love themselves and others.

Part #3 — Retrain your Thinking

Your thinking is the computer that constructs your beliefs and drives your words and behavior. Thoughts create corresponding behavior, and you must change your thinking in order to change your beliefs, behavior, and emotions.

This means that you can identify a specific behavior in yourself, target it by identifying the thoughts and beliefs behind the behavior, and change those thoughts. You can actually identify, remove, and insert new thoughts on specific topics that create undesirable behavior.

You have heard, that behind every good man is a good woman? Well, I would also say that behind every good or bad behavior is a good or bad thought. If you change your thoughts specifically or in a general attitudinal way, then you change your decision making and thus the outcome in your life.

You can actually remove the bad and insert the good thoughts in your mind on purpose and by design. You can remove and replace the old unwanted, negative, or destructive patterns with new productive patterns that are capable of producing your own desired results. You have that creative ability inside of you.

I have learned that in order to be healthy and maximize our potential in life, we must all go through this process. Some people go through this process discreetly and privately on their own through counseling, church attendance, confessions, prayer, and by other means.

In the Trinity Program, we take people through this process in an organized, professional, and powerful way. We address the tri-union of the human, which is the spirit (the heart), soul (the mind, will, and emotions), and the body (the physical body you occupy as a spirit being). You are a spirit, you occupy your physical body, and you have a mind and emotions.

Our will is the part of our spirit and mind that gives us the ability to make choices. Another way of saying this is that every person has the God-given authority to choose and make decisions. Your will is a part of your spirit and is processed through your mind. You must submit your will, act out your decisions, and those decisions will either bless or curse you. I will address this topic in more detail in the following chapters.

Once you have completed this process, you are in a place where you can be healthy and whole and can maximize your God-given potential.

> **Pursue knowledge from people who are living life better than you are in any regard. It means that they must know something you do not know. It also means that you can have what they have!**

There is a measurable process that you will go through when you are healing and maximizing your potential. Consistent with my Trinity Program curriculum, I have provided the following simple flow chart that will help you measure where you are at any given point in your growth process:

1) Confession and repentance: Confession requires the use of your spoken words. Spoken words should access the area of a wound that you are targeting and referencing and provide a release of the emotions, sensations, and pain that is associated or was associated with that wound.

During confession, the wound must be identified and labeled. Confession should also describe how that wounding experience affected you and what it did to you. Confession is an essential part of repentance, which is another word for change. It exposes the wound and behaviors related to the experience and that removes the secrecy of it.

I often say that secrecy is one of the greatest enablers of any negative or destructive behavior. Negative or destructive behavior can include acts of lying, stealing, manipulation, physical abuse, embezzlement, alcohol or substance abuse, compulsive spending, murder, etc.

Deviancy is also a destructive behavior, but is a violation in a category of its own, in that it violates the sexuality and identity of a person, because of the intimate contact or penetration of the body, soul, or spirit it creates. It can violate and alter your purity and self-image (what you think about yourself/see yourself). Deviant sexual acts can victimize and wound, even if they are self-induced.

Repentance is a removal of the old and a replacement of the new (heart and behavior change).

2) Forgiveness: Forgive God (many people have unforgiveness against God because of a trauma and belief that God abandoned them and they hold it against Him), self (release the debt against yourself), and others. Forgiveness is also receiving forgiveness.

Leave it, let it go, and release it so that the bitterness will not infect your soul and cause you to become someone you do not desire to be or think you could become. The venomous outcome of trapped emotional toxins inside of you will turn you into the opposite of God's creation of you. Darkness will take over your soul the longer you harbor negative emotions such as unforgiveness, bitterness, resentment, hate, rage, offense, murder, criticalness, grieving, self-loathing, etc. You must release it for your own health sake first.

These destructive emotions will also ruin the good relationships you want to maintain, and will eventually make you physically unhealthy and transform your youth into pre-mature old age. Even your very appearance will be altered. The unresolved past is unhealthy for you and you cannot handle it. It can and will destroy you.

> **Trapped emotional toxins inside of you will turn you into the opposite of God's creation of you.**

Forgiveness sometimes requires that you "by faith" just go ahead and say you forgive so that you can begin the process with those words. Spoken words are a way you release something you don't want and receive something you do want. This is true even if you don't feel the forgiveness and release at that moment.

Remember, you are not a hypocrite if you, by faith, say you forgive and you don't feel it right then. Forgiveness begins with a decision, not an emotion.

3) Deliverance and healing: Deliverance from oppressive strongholds and demonic activity involves the exposure and cleansing of the wounds (hurts, betrayals, rejections, abandonment's, divorces, abortion, adultery, rape, death, etc.).

4) Removing old patterns: Identify and label the patterns correctly, then stop them, invalidate them (decide they are no longer a valid behavior), and do not practice them.

5) Replacing old patterns with new productive ones: After you remove the old patterns, you denounce them (sever the bond and create separation). Then you identify the new patterns you want, validate those patterns (decide they are valid behaviors), receive and bond with them.

6) Practice the new productive patterns: Practicing new patterns until they become automatic requires a minimum of six months retraining. They will then become a part of your new identity.

7) Wholeness: This is when all healthy parts are working together. Practice until the new replacement behaviors integrate into your entire system (spirit, soul, and body) and are accepted as "normal."

8) Healthy relationships: Choose relationships that bless and not curse you, that empower and not hinder you, that are not a trauma bond (see trauma bonding section).

9) Maximizing your God-given gifts and personality strengths: This is your potential. Identify your gifts and strengths, develop them, use them, and they will work for you. They never go away.

10) Write down your vision: What is your vision for the next six months and the next five years? Write it down.

11) Implement the vision: Practical steps to walk it out.

12) Stay your course: You have a plan, now you walk it out, modifying as appropriate.

13) Complete the vision: This is where you reap your harvest.

I want you to always remember that failure is an attitude, not an experience! Situational failure and trials will be inevitable if you are actively pursuing your purpose in life. If you fail, get back up and place yourself right back into your designed vision.

History reveals that the great Abraham Lincoln failed many times in his attempts to be elected for political office. He finally succeeded and changed the course of this nation forever.

When fear of failure speaks to you, do not believe its message, even if it is an internal struggle. You will learn that fear lies; that it is never your ally and will never promote God's potential inside of you.

God's potential will always prevail. Place yourself into the potential that He put inside of you in the form of your God-given giftings and personality strengths. Your giftings will never fail you. They will always create fulfillment and success. Your job is to develop and use them, and God's job is to make them produce results for you. God will always do His part.

What people are saying about the Trinity Program:

> *The Trinity Program was offered to me at a time in my life when I was feeling overwhelmed, out of control and angry much of the time. I was not happy with my actions and the way I was treating my family and neglecting myself. I needed a "therapeutic getaway!" The Trinity program was that and so much more! It was quaint, relaxing, intense, refreshing and life-changing. I cannot explain in words the anointing that was present and the way it touched me. I am glad to say I will never be the same. Praise be to God!*
> — Michelle (San Antonio, TX)

> *The Trinity Program goes far beyond "typical" Christian therapy sessions or even a Biblical retreat. Aside from the tranquil setting, the delectable menu and the profound teaching, this program is life-transforming because it equips you with the training and discipline that we may have missed receiving in our youth. I have been freed to draw*

near to God and to help others do the same. I can now forget what is behind and look forward to my calling in Christ Jesus.
— N.S. (San Antonio, TX)

It was life-changing…the two things I got most out of the Trinity Program were the further education outside of appointment time with Dr. Jones, coupled with the bonding experiences with the other people there. I was so touched and moved by the life-experiences that people had and shared with the group. It's like an appointment with Dr. Jones multiplied by a hundred!
— T.L.C. (San Antonio, TX)

Through the Trinity Program, Dr. Jones helped me to process my past and set aside my old way of thinking. I realized that my thoughts were so clouded that it affected my perspective on every aspect of my life, including my spiritual walk. The Trinity Program also helped me to restore my identity in Christ and on that foundation I have made a conscious effort to stay on the path of renewing my mind every day and maintaining a healthy approach to life.
— M.M. (Cincinnati, OH)

Chapter 2

Learned Behavior

Learned behavior is developed by practicing thoughts, beliefs, behaviors, and emotions over a period of time. The learned behavior becomes a habit and eventually automatic behaviors set in.

It is a conditioning process and occurs whether the behavior is productive or destructive, positive or negative. Behavior moves into the beginning stages of a habit after about 30 days of practice and becomes automatic after about six months of practice.

Here are some facts to consider:

- Automatic behavior is a behavior that is downloaded from the conscious to the subconscious to the unconscious mind and is defined as something that you think, say, or do without conscious, premeditated thought at the time of the behavior.

- Habit is a behavior that functions on the subconscious level and is a pattern but is not yet automatic.

- A pattern is a series of recurring thoughts or behaviors that forms a certain recurring way of thinking or doing, typically with the same end-results.

The following sequence explains the cycle of learned behavior:

Thoughts > Beliefs > Actions > Emotions > Habit > Character

Prolonged thoughts produce beliefs, emotions, and eventual behavior. I have broken down the different aspects of behavior and defined them so that you can understand and apply them to your life:

THOUGHTS ...

Thoughts are made up of all mental activity that is practiced as a body of ideas, memories, processing, decisions, imaginations, personality, perceptions, self-image, self-worth, conscience, desires, and learning. It is associated with certain times in history (past), the present (real time), or the future. *Webster's New World College Edition* says that thoughts include the power of reasoning, conceiving ideas, mental engrossment, preoccupation, or concentration.

Thoughts establish beliefs and create behavior and corresponding emotions. Therefore, thoughts possess an important purpose in our lives, for without thoughts you would not have beliefs, behavioral intelligence, or emotions.

Thoughts are also learned. When you were born you had one level of mental activity and learned to walk, talk, act, respond, hold a spoon, crawl, ride a bike, write, calculate, and more.

Your thoughts also produce corresponding words. Words and behavior are not accidental because they originate in your thoughts.

Thoughts create behavior.

Some thoughts are positive and some are negative, and those thoughts create positive or negative corresponding behavior. When you try to convince yourself that your behavior was accidental and it "just happened," you are trying to believe a clinical untruth because behavior comes from thoughts.

When you want to really recognize and know someone, or even yourself, observe both words and behavior. Don't just observe them separately. If the words and behavior are contrary to each other, then you know that the person's thoughts are in conflict.

Spoken words are also behavior. Both words and other physical behavior will reveal your thought life. In fact, all behavior is a reflection of your thoughts. Behavior is not accidental. It is a product of prolonged thoughts and beliefs.

Behavior in the form of words and physical actions/responses is a product of your previous thoughts. If the two line up with each other, then your mind is consistent and not deceptive. If they do not line up with consistency, then the thoughts are different than the behavior and there is deception, secrecy, denial, or at least avoidance.

Remember, secrecy is the greatest enabler of any destructive or negative behavior. If you are in a dating relationship with someone who avoids, hides information, lies, deceives, or maintains a secret lifestyle or existence, then confront that person immediately and cut off that relationship. You cannot strive for someone else's improvement more than they do for themselves!

Thoughts must be managed and must not be allowed to create just any scenario in your mind. Those unbridled thoughts can become destructive if you have no boundaries. If you develop your thoughts and manage them well, you can learn to achieve greatness, and most importantly, fulfill your God-given potential.

It is important that you understand this profound and unchanging truth about thoughts:

> If you change your thoughts (thinking)
> on any topic, then your beliefs and behavior
> will be changed and transformed.

There is a direct correlation between your thoughts, beliefs, words, and behavior. You are changed by the changing of your thoughts. If you keep the same thoughts, then you will keep the same beliefs and behavior. If you change your thoughts, you will change your beliefs and behavior.

You must never allow yourself to justify thoughts simply because they are your thoughts and you are familiar with them. This type of assumption is founded in pride and will become a stumbling block as you attempt to improve your life. You must truthfully evaluate whether or not your thoughts are producing your desired results based upon your potential and strengths.

If your desired results are not being attained, then that means your thoughts need to be corrected and modified to produce your intended results! You will only produce better results if you first change your thinking. It is not enough to merely agree that your thinking needs to be changed. Instead, you must identify and label accurately the exact wrong thinking that is the culprit. Then target it, remove it, and replace it with the new productive thoughts that will produce your desired results. The new thinking must be by design and on purpose.

You must then test your new thinking by practicing it, even though it may be unfamiliar territory and uncomfortable for a while. Just because you are uncomfortable does not mean the discomfort is warning you of danger in some way. Often, discomfort is a sign that something has changed and you are experiencing unknowns. In spite of the unknown and unfamiliar territory, the change can be the start of a productive transformation.

> **Results are the only accurate measuring tool for productive change.**

Results are the only accurate measuring tool for productive change. Feelings are not the measuring tool for productive change. Do not believe your feelings just because you have them. The feelings are yours and they are real, maybe even very powerful, but they can make you unpredictable, inconsistent, and distract you from your new productive behavioral pathway. Again, results are the only accurate measuring tool to verify your positive transformation.

Productive thoughts will always produce productive behavioral results. Results are another word for "fruit." The seed of thought will eventually produce the corresponding fruit of behavior: good or bad, right or wrong, productive or destructive, positive or negative, etc.

You must also realize that thoughts can be productive, good, and positive but still not maximize your potential. Thoughts can be good and still limit you. You may not hurt anyone, do good deeds, and produce some good fruit in life, but you will still only be using a portion of the ground in the orchard and a portion of the seed in your hand.

It has been said that "good" is the enemy of "better" and better is the enemy of "best." Do not crown yourself in victory just because you are doing average in life and you are not hurting anyone and have a mediocre job. Examine your potential and dreams in life. Identity them and write them down. Put a six-month and five-year plan together to attain those dreams and goals. Begin to pursue your dreams even if you have to take baby steps.

Cross the action barrier instead of just thinking about it. If your thoughts are full of fear, doubt, unbelief, torment, insecurity, uncertainty, and lack of knowledge, then begin to reform your thoughts by first dreaming. Use your imagination and draw out scenarios in your mind of where you want to be and what you want to be. Get that picture in your mind and you have begun the process of change. That new picture in your imagination will serve as the new model that will be your reference point for future behavior, change, and new results in your life. Thoughts will then turn into action. Too many people realize, and even agree, that they need help, and agree on the help you say they need. However, they feel a sense of accomplishment because they came this far, but then do not take action and consequently can't improve because action is required to improve. An agreement without taking action on it is dead, and powerless to help you. You must take action before you can achieve results. You can't just have thoughts about it. You must act, even if you are uncomfortable with acting. Do it and the comfort will eventually come.

In order to act out a new behavior, you must first have a picture of your behavioral model in your mind. You can design that new model by using the imagination that was given to you by God for "vision." Vision is a mental image that portrays your desired results and even the pathway to get those results. That image can be general or detailed, depending on how much thought you put into it.

Allow yourself to dream and spend some time on it. If fear and doubt creep in, just let them pass on by and get right back to your vision for the future. Designing this kind of image in your mind can be accomplished even if you don't have past successes related to your vision and dreams for the future. Just design the image. Start there and you have begun the process of change.

Vision is required for any long-term change because it serves as your reference point and guide to stay on track so you won't stray off course by the distractions of other mediocre people and your own emotional insecurities and uncertainties. Remember, emotions are not your guide. Emotions will fluctuate. Emotions have a purpose, but they are not intended by God to lead you. Use your thoughts to create an image of your dreams. Make it clear and write it down. There is power in writing and declaring your vision and making it clear.

> **Change your thoughts ... and change is guaranteed.**

Remember, transformed thoughts will transform you. If you try to change your behavior while leaving your thoughts the same, you will only be developing short-term behavior modification rather than long-term change. Long-term change requires change of thought. If you modify your behavior and do not change your core thinking and beliefs about that behavior, you will become "double-minded," deceptive, and unstable. A double-minded person is one who has shifting thoughts that create shifting behavior. Another way of saying this is that unstable thoughts create unstable behavior.

Are you panicking or discouraged right now? Are you thinking that maybe you are not ready or mature enough in your thinking to institute this kind of change? If so, you must decide right now to find someone who can help you improve your thinking. Find someone who is more successful and more knowledgeable than you in the area of your desired change. Do not get advice from someone who has never succeeded in this area. Ask for help and be ready and willing to listen and learn. The Scripture says that only a fool does not listen to instruction.

You will find that most people are willing to help you if you will just ask. Ask for help even if you feel afraid. Remember, fear does not tell you the truth. It will make you feel like there is danger of rejection, non-acceptance, or too much vulnerability. But you must push through the fear and pursue knowledge and help, even when you are afraid.

Do not obey the fear. It will always limit you and eventually put you in a box that provides a false sense of safety from exposure. Step outside the box and take the perceived risk. Scripture says that when you seek you shall find, when you knock it shall be opened unto you, that you have not because you ask not, and that if you ask you shall receive.

Thought is a form of seed and seed always produces corresponding fruit. Without seed, it is impossible to have corresponding fruit. Scripture also says that whatsoever a man sows, that and that only is what he will reap (Galatians 6:7). The seed of thought will always produce corresponding fruit (results) of behavior.

As a counselor, I am often asked if I can guarantee that thoughts will transform a person's behavior. My answer is always, "Yes!"

The reason I can confidently guarantee that this principle works every time is because it is a universal law upon which all behavior and results are governed. Seed planted in the ground produces corresponding fruit. All inventions start out with a conceived idea from thought and eventually become a tangible reality. Every tangible product that man has ever developed started out with the seed of thought. Every highway, car, airplane, hat, shoe, watch, cup, satellite, printer, computer, phone, book, and more, began in the form of a thought. Everything that exists began with a thought.

It should be obvious to you that the law of sowing and reaping works. It always works. The fact is that you cannot stop this law from working. It will work for you or against you, but it will always work. I am encouraging you to understand it and put it to work for you!

BELIEFS ...

A belief is any information that is received into the mind or heart that becomes established as truth. Beliefs produce and promote behavior. People act out what they believe and usually do not violate their own beliefs, unless they have doubt about those beliefs.

Unfortunately, people develop beliefs or allow other people to develop their own beliefs that produce destructive behavior. Never allow someone else to develop your beliefs unless those people are successful in that area of achievement themselves. You do not want someone who is still sabotaging their marriage with destructive thinking and behaviors to give you marriage advice. Most likely the beliefs they have are not good ones and will lead you astray and produce the same results in your life, precisely the ones you do not want.

Consequently, you have to evaluate the level of competency and success in the person you allow to speak into your life. As I previously stated, I strongly suggest that you pursue people who are doing it well or at least as good as you are. Find people who have succeeded where you want to succeed and listen to their advice.

Beliefs enforce and justify behavior, whether good or bad, and some beliefs fluctuate (i.e. lying under certain circumstances is okay but not under other circumstances). Nevertheless, they are still abiding by their beliefs.

You have beliefs about everything you do and do not do. You have beliefs about God, parenting, morals, relationships, money, behavior, marriage, children, self-worth, age, animals, education, exercise, potential, secrecy, sports, your past, and much more. You name it — you have a belief about it.

Your beliefs dictate your behavior, boundaries, and actions. Beliefs even affect your emotions. If you believe that you are unsafe, you will not open up and allow yourself to love or receive love. On the other hand, if you believe you are safe, you will open up and allow positive feelings to be generated in regard to that person, place, or thing.

Examine your beliefs and understand what and why you believe like you do. If those beliefs are hindering your potential in life, then change those specific beliefs and retain the ones that empower your God-given potential.

ACTIONS ...

Action is an act or response. It constitutes behavior that is acted outwardly (physical activity and motion) or internally (thought activity and emotions). *Webster's* defines action as "the doing of something; state of being in motion or in working."

A person can act on a behavior whether that behavior is obvious and overt or unobvious and covert. Spoken words, body posture, smiles, eye motion, eye contact, and sounds (sighs) are all included in action. Actions are therefore any physical motion or behavior and can also include responses and reactions. Responses are usually planned behaviors that are thought out. *Webster's* defines a response as, "something said or done in answer…"

Responses are usually more productive answers and reactions less thought out and more impulsive. Additionally, responses are not impulsive but are pre-programmed and purposeful. Reactions actually may be thought about and justified in advance, but are not filtered at the time they are activated. *Webster's* defines reaction as, "a return or apposing action, force, influence, etc."

Fear actions and responses are a type of wound behavior that many people struggle with. There are various types of fear, such as fear of the unknown, intimacy, social settings, personal exposure, inadequacies, and more. Fear-based control is always used to reduce the anxiety caused by fear. Therefore, some kind of control is used to make the person feel less vulnerable, less exposed, more protected, and safer.

The control is also used to reduce the "unknowns" and create as many "knowns" as possible in an attempt to not have fear of the unknown. When control is violated or threatened in some way, the person usually feels one of three fears:

1) Fear of being controlled.
2) Fear of being out of control.
3) Fear of not being in control.

When controls are threatened in these ways, then fear increases along with the stress, anxiety, and even panic that accompanies control being violated in one or more of these three ways. Controls are mechanisms that make people feel like they are protected from what they are afraid of.

Fear-based control mechanisms are used to compensate for vulnerabilities and insecurities so that they won't feel weak and have the potential to be hurt again. The problem is that these same mechanisms control the one that thinks they are being protected by the controls and they never really can open up and receive love in an emotionally close and intimate way. If control cannot be gained, then the controller will experience some level of stress or anxiety. Control is used in order for the controller to feel better. The controller may have a self-worth wound that produces feelings of being invaluable if people do not obey, no matter how unreasonable the demands might be.

Control does not always have to be rational and is not. Consider these examples:

- A friend gets mad at a friend who is simply being nice to someone else.
- A mother who gets angry at her son for having one hair out of place and she shows displeasure to him because he did not get it right.
- A dad who will not spend quality time with his children because he controls them with silence and distancing so he will not be exposed and have to open up in some personal and intimate way.
- A wife who was violated sexually as a teenager and now controls all of, or certain affection, with her husband so that she will not feel controlled, out of control, or not in control. If she isn't in control, then the exposure represents too much vulnerability and she feels unprotected and unsafe. Therefore she does not open up to her husband nor can she really enjoy closeness with him. Of course this also creates frustration in the husband and he

can begin to feel unwanted and rejected as a result of the control that originated from an unresolved wound in her and the fears that follow.

Guilt motivation is also often used to control people. Guilt motivation is when controllers accuse their victims of doing something wrong for the purpose of inducing guilt so that the victims will do what the controllers demand (more on guilt motivation in the Retraining the Mind section).

Actions that are practiced over a prolonged period of time will be encoded into your central nervous system and muscle memory as normal and automatic programmed behavior. This is a law of learned behavior and will work whether the behavior is good or bad, productive or destructive.

EMOTIONS ...

Emotions include all mental or bodily senses, bodily energy, feelings, excitement, sensations, and expressions. A feeling is often defined as an emotion as well. However, feelings are usually identified as related to the body, while emotions usually are related to the central nervous system expressions.

Energy generates through the central nervous system and is felt inside the body. This is accompanied by internal thought messages and impulses, like passion, anger, hurt, fear, rejection, etc.

Emotions can also be remembered in the body (muscle memory) and central nervous system (emotional memory).

HABIT ...

A habit develops after you practice a behavior for approximately 30 days, give or take a few days (I allow for different personality types and consistency). A habit is a pattern of behavior that develops because that specific behavior is practiced over this period of time. It downloads from the conscious to the subconscious mind and can be described as just below the surface of your conscious processing and reality.

A habit is also a behavior that is past tense because it has been practiced. Encoding in the brain, central nervous system, and muscles is occurring as the behavior is developed into a pattern. A habit is also the beginning of the neurological pathway construction, which is known as "brain elasticity."

Automatic Behavior

Character is also called "automatic" behavior and both are seen as "second nature." Automatic behavior is a behavior that has been practiced until it downloads into the unconscious mind. Automatic behavior requires a minimum six months of practicing that specific behavior before it moves into the beginning stages of automatic.

Automatic behavior is encoded into the unconscious mind. I define it as something you think, say, or do without conscious, premeditated intent at the time of the behavior. This stage of behavior development or change is the final stage of the neurological pathway construction. This means that when a behavior is practiced, neurological pathways are constructed because you are practicing. The neurological pathways are like highways that accommodate traffic. The pathways accommodate the firing and flow of neurotransmitters that are fired by neurons full of energy. As the neurons fire, they create pathways that are connected by "synapses" which bind together the sections of the highway. These highways accommodate the behavior that you are practicing.

> **It takes 30 days to develop a habit.**

You can remember it this way: WHAT FIRES, WIRES. Your most frequently acted out behavior begins to wire and eventually becomes automatic behavior that flows naturally without making yourself act it out.

The Human System

God created us as complex living beings. We are made up of a "system" that is spirit, mind, emotions, and body. All four parts work together synergistically to function as one whole. If all of the parts of the system are healthy and functioning in their designed purpose, then the entire system can work together in wholeness.

Unhealthy parts require other parts of the system to overcompensate and suffer for the deficiencies and unhealthiness of those parts. An unhealthy mind will negatively affect the body through physical destructiveness, abuse, or neglect to the body. An unhealthy or dead spirit will affect the mind, emotions, and body by carrying the burdens of past wounds, hurts, and pain. Unhealthy emotions will impulsively escalate a person into an offense to lash out without being able to intervene or prevent the escalation. Unhealthy emotions also create unpredictability, moods, and hypersensitivity. Unhealthy emotions also create self-medicating with comfort food, overspending, alcohol, drug abuse, and more.

I describe our human system (which is commonly described as spirit, soul, and body) as a divinely molded and bound together union of four parts, which include:

#1 — The spirit

This is the real us, the original created part of God that was breathed into man's physical body that will always remain in existence after the body dies. The spirit can be fed/unfed, nurtured/not nurtured, clean/dirty, ruled/unruly, righteous/evil, cultivated/uncultivated, soft/hard, alive/dead, light/dark, willing/unwilling, stirred/unstirred, serving/not serving, repentant/unrepentant, proud/humble, desirous/not desirous, but it is always eternal. Your spirit sees beyond the physical realm.

#2 — The mind (a part of the soul)

With direction of thinking, the mind includes all thought activity and is also called the psyche, from which we get the word psychology. The mind is made of what I call "arenas" of the mind which include the following categories: intellect (processing, decisions, reasoning), learning (acquire, get knowledge, understand), memory (reference points from learning, accept, store and recall information), personality (behavioral characteristics or strengths and weaknesses which identify a person's uniqueness), desires (wish, long for, crave, covet, strong appetite), conscience (discern the difference between right and wrong, moral sense or judgment, ethics) and beliefs (information received and accepted as truth).

#3 — The emotions (a part of the soul)

These are feelings and sensations initiated by thoughts and generated throughout the central nervous system and the body. They are also stored as memory in the brain (emotional and picture memory), body (muscle memory), bodily organs, and the central nervous system (encoded as behavioral "programs").

#4 — The body

This includes the whole physical substance of a human being, physical mass or body, flesh, bones, organs, physical motion, physical expressions and experiences, physical existence, physical evidence, and bodily material substance.

The reason it is important to describe our system is to state that this entire human system can learn, memorize, and express itself synergistically based upon its health and programming. If each part of this entire system is healthy and is working together as created, then the person is a "whole" person.

This type of condition does not happen accidentally or just because more time passes by. Rather, it happens because a person decides to be healthy and whole, even at the risk of failure. It takes work and cannot be achieved alone. Everyone needs help and everyone needs God. There are no exceptions.

BEHAVIORAL LAWS AFFECT YOU

Learned behavior is a conditioned and developed behavior that operates on or is governed by certain "laws" of behavior that apply to every living human being on every level and every part of the human's system. These laws also govern all four parts of the human system that I just described.

This means that a created spirit (the real you) can grow in knowledge, maturity, and closeness with God. The human spirit can also decline and separate from God. The point is that even the spirit of a man is able to respond. It is not a lifeless blob of nothing. Every person will remain spiritually in existence somewhere for eternity. Someone wisely stated, "There was a day that you were not, but there will never again be a day that you will not be." Learned behavior applies to entire union of the spirit, mind, emotions, and body, and it has the ability to learn behavior and express it. Another way of saying this is that a person can learn and express behavior on a spiritual, mental, emotional, and physical level!

All human behavior operates on laws of behavior. I call these laws the Law of the Mind and The Law of Action. Laws are like gravity. They work the same way every day and are no respecter of persons. Regardless of how important or unimportant you are, these laws work the same.

This, of course, means that if you learn them then they can help you … and if you do not learn them or you resist them then they can hurt you. One truth always remains the same, and that is that these laws of the universe of behavior will never change just for you. You are not the exception in the universe, contrary to any delusions you might have or denials you are practicing.

Consider these laws:

- **The Law of the Mind**: prolonged thoughts produce beliefs, corresponding emotions, and eventual physical behavior and physical motion/activity.

- **The Law of Action**: prolonged action (internal, external) downloads in the mind, creates neurological pathways and also encodes into the central nervous system and muscle memory as normal. They become "programs" that are activated when triggered with present-tense experiences or memories or brain associations.

It is the transmission of energy in the direction of the behavior that creates these highways through which internal files flow. By the time a neurological pathway fully develops, the behavior will be automatic. So if a person learns to ride a bicycle and practices the behavior of riding, that practice will develop neurological pathways through which that learned behavior will automatically flow. Even if there is a break in the practicing, the information is still encoded and stored and can be used again when activated. Your system will remember how to do it. You may need some practice to fine tune it, but the pathways are encoded and can be accessed by doing it again.

I am often asked as a counselor, how long it takes to change a behavior. Concerned spouses want to see change in their relationship, or parents need to be equipped to train their children, or individuals want to change their own behavior. The answer is that it takes about 30 days for a new behavior to move into the beginning stages of "habit" and about six months for a new behavior to become character (or automatic behavior).

The new behavior must be practiced consistently for these time periods to be accurate. If you just practice your changes periodically and with little or no enthusiasm, the time period for change will, of course, be longer. A friend once asked me, "If you knew you would make one million dollars at the end of one year, would you work on that project every day without fail for that year?"

The laws apply to everyone, everywhere, all the time.

Who would say no to that? Then I realized that if people are sincere about their change and personal improvement, but are not willing to do what it takes on a consistent basis, then the change isn't going to happen. Change does not happen accidentally, and it is not very easy. In order to change, you must not think in terms of it being hard or easy. You must think in terms of doing what it takes to get your desired results. The 30 day and six month time periods take into consideration differing personality types and varying levels of effort, so give or take a few days, these time periods are accurate.

If you want to change, you must identify what you want to remove and stop practicing it. Then you must identify the replacement thinking and behavior and practice it with conviction until that new behavior becomes habit and eventually character (automatic).

Addictions:

In the case of addictions, the time period required for change is extended. With addictions, a new habit forms in about six months and character (automatic behavior) forms in about one to three years. This is why it takes "treatment" to deal with and conquer addictions.

As we've discussed, when a habit is formed there are neurotransmitters firing in the direction of that new behavior, causing neurological pathways to be formed. During this construction time, there is a pattern of behavior being developed, but the behavior is not yet automatic. The new behavior is, however, getting easier to practice.

Habit is thoughts and behavior that are just below the surface of the conscious level thought world that function in the present tense. Character or automatic behavior is also called "past tense" because it developed in the past tense (but reinforced by practicing in the present) and operates on the unconscious level of the mind. This simply means that the thoughts and central nervous system memory are producing that behavior automatically, without conscious, premeditated thought at the time of the behavior.

This explanation is necessary again because not only is there learned behavior involved with addictions, but also chemistry in the brain that is often altered and imbalanced in addition to the behavioral side of the addiction. There is no shame in pursuing the help you need if you are suffering from an addiction. There will be shame involved in not receiving help because the addiction will NOT remain secret forever.

It will expose itself and you will not be able to continue living in that secret world that enables your bondage forever. You will intervene into it and dismantle it or it will dismantle you.

Addictions consist of thoughts, central nervous system encoding, behavior, and chemistry (neurotransmitters and hormones), which create patterns, cravings, and withdrawals if the body, mind, and emotions do not receive its stimulation or relief from the torment of the addiction. Addictions do "torment" people, not just the addicted, but everyone in the relationship. According to the medical encyclopedia, an addiction is a dependence on a behavior or substance that a person is powerless to stop. There is also a difference between "substance" (drugs, alcohol) and "behavior" (gambling, pornography) addictions.

Addictions can develop in many ways. An addiction usually starts out with some form of self-medicating for the purpose of reducing or relieving high levels of stress, anxiety, panic, or pain. Eventually, that self-medicating can turn into an addiction and the person becomes dependent upon it to have some relief from the agony.

> **If you don't beat your addiction, your addiction will beat you.**

There are numerous forms of self-medicating which include some of the following substances or behaviors: alcohol, drugs (chemicals), sex, pornography (fantasy through which there is no rejection, no commitment demands, arguing, and elevated self-esteem because you are always good enough and in total control), spending, gambling, eating, obsessive working out/exercise, over-working, attention-getting (dancing, emotional drama, seductive dressing, arguing, threats to hurt one's self, announcing their successes, loud talking), busy work (to preoccupy the mind), etc.

Of course all self-medicating does not form addictions, but you will know if you are addicted on a substance because you are dependent on it to make you feel better and you will be thinking about it too often. An addiction will eventually rule your life with cravings and emotional, mental, and bodily torment. The torment will not stop until you have relieved yourself.

This is why you are in bondage because it rules you and you are its slave and it is your master. Whatever you serve is your master.

Section II

The Laws that Govern You

All seed produces corresponding fruit. It is impossible to have fruit without a previous seed being planted. Seed planted in the ground and watered, will always produce a harvest. The seed of thought will always produce corresponding fruit called behavior ... corresponding fruit, not different fruit. Watermelon seed will not produce corn. Thoughts about cars will not develop your muscles. Practicing thoughts by acting on them is another word for watering the seed. Therefore behavior is not accidental. Behavior exists for a reason and has an origination point. It is either pre-meditated before the behavior or learned (programmed) or a genetic characteristic. Behavior that is practiced will be developed and always gets easier, stronger and more automatic. "Practice makes perfect."

These laws operate in two domains: the spiritual and the natural. The spiritual condition of a person affects the mind, emotions, and body. The mental, emotional, and physical condition of a person affects the spiritual. These are the laws that govern everything that was ever made and all behavior. The seed of thought, turned into tangible reality, produced hats, roads, clothes, cars, buses, satellites, glasses, telephones, tables, guns, concrete, printers, and everything else that was ever made by humans. The same law governs all behavior and its results or consequences. This is a law from which you cannot escape. You can bless or curse, help or hurt yourself with it, but this law will always exist. It is the Law of Sowing and Reaping.

Chapter 3

The Law of the Mind

The Law of the Mind is a behavioral law that applies to thoughts and the beliefs, behavior, and emotions created by thought. Prolonged thought will eventually lead to beliefs and those beliefs will eventually produce and justify behaviors.

All people act on what they believe, whether those beliefs are productive or destructive, good or bad, silent or open. Once you believe something, it is hard to get you to violate or abandon those beliefs. This is one reason it is so important to know what you believe and to not validate and protect a belief that does not produce positive behavior and good fruit in your life.

You must realize that you have the authority and power to insert, by design, certain beliefs into your belief system. Beliefs always produce corresponding behavior. Beliefs come from your thoughts and from experiences that you have. However, let me warn you to never establish negative beliefs about God during a trial, trauma, or crisis in your life. He has not abandoned you.

Why what fires, wires

Neurotransmitters are chemical substances that account for the transmission of signals from one neuron to the next across synapses (connectors between cells and neurons).

Neurons connect the nervous systems and respond to stimuli (activity and action) and communicate the presence of stimuli to the central nervous system that processes that information and sends responses to other parts of the body for action. Medications and amino acid supplements, used to treat depression, anxiety, and other chemical imbalances, usually target the neurotransmitters. Dopamine, as an example, may be related to social anxiety when in low supply, so some researchers say. Serotonin is also involved in moods and your mind "distorting" when you are under pressure.

Neurotransmitters transmit nerve impulses throughout the entire human nervous system, which includes the Central Nervous System (brain and spinal cord), Peripheral Nervous System (everything else related to sensory and motor in the brain and spinal cord), Somatic Nervous System (sense organs and skeletal muscles), Autonomic Nervous System (muscles and glands), Sympathetic Motor System (fight or flight responses), and Parasympathetic System (relaxing responses).

These neurotransmitters, therefore, affect pleasures, excitement, fight or flight responses, memory, learning, emotions, moods, depression, panic, anxiety, anxiousness, OCD characteristics, quick temper, anger, trouble sleeping, perceptions, and even suicide tendencies.

All of this means that the most frequently acted out behavior on any topic/subject causes neurotransmitters (energy sources) to fire in the direction of that behavior. These transmitters have connectors (synapses) that construct the pathways and highways that will accommodate behavior when it first develops, and promote or enable that behavior to eventually become automatic behavior.

Therefore, what you practice in your thought world and in your actions, will fire neurotransmitters which develop neuro-highways that accommodate the behavior and make it easier and more automatic the longer you practice it.

You can see how important it is to know what you practice, not just what you MEANT to do. Pay attention to what you say and do, not what you MEANT to say and do. Focus your self-corrections on what you actually say and do. Pray and ask God to help you be aware of your own behaviors.

SHORT-TERM CHANGES

Many of us have been able to make short-term changes, breaking out of a destructive thought pattern for a period of time. But if the change in thinking patterns is short-term, the corresponding behavior change will also be short-term. You must evaluate if you are willing to do what it takes to change and improve long-term. You can agree that you need to change and even say that you want to, but the final proof that you are willing and want to, is if you actually finish it out.

That's why so many people go on a "diet" and lose weight, only to gain it back again. Diets are by nature short-term behavior modification. The only long-lasting results in weight loss or health management come from a change in lifestyle out of desperation or intense desire, which starts out with a change in thoughts and beliefs and becomes behavior when it is practiced until it is ingrained, along with the thoughts into our character, as automatic.

When you change your thoughts, you must force yourself to practice the corresponding behavior until the new thoughts and behavior become automatic.

When you understand the Law of the Mind, you can put it to work for you. Start reprogramming your thought patterns, renewing your mind, and make a decision that your change in thinking will be a permanent one. When you do that, only one thing can happen: your change in thinking will bring about new, lasting emotional and behavioral changes that will produce the results you desire.

If you work on your thought world, you will get the results manifested in your behavior. If you do the work, it will work for you. Remember, when you change your thoughts, you must then force yourself (if necessary) to practice the physical corresponding behavior until the new thoughts and behavior become automatic.

Where is this principle in the Bible? Romans 12:2 says; "...be transformed (changed) by the renewing of your mind...." It is a Bible truth that you need to work on your thought world in order to change your mindset, your outlook on life, and your outcome.

When you change your thoughts and make new decisions, you must force yourself to practice the new behavior with action, until your new thoughts and behavior become automatic.

As I mentioned before, it is possible and even common, to change your thoughts but still not experience lasting behavioral change. The reason for this disappointing outcome is because you simply did not cross the "action barrier" and behaviorally put into practice your new decisions. I say again, thoughts that are practiced over time will download from the conscious level of the mind to the subconscious and eventually to the unconscious. Thoughts that are unwanted and that produce unwanted behaviors and emotions must be "red flagged," noticed, and automatically "obeyed."

The Law of the Mind guarantees that those practiced thoughts will become automatic thoughts and eventually behavior. Once you recognize unwanted, negative, or destructive thoughts (ways of thinking), you must decide that those thoughts are no longer valid or acceptable so that you can intervene, or even prevent them in advance. Then replace them with new thoughts and behaviors and keep practicing and renewing your mind to them until it gets easier. Remember the old phrase: "practice makes perfect." That does not mean that you will be perfect, but it does mean that you can do it with excellence, ease, and comfort. The more you practice, the easier and more comfortable you will be with it, and the more efficient you will become. Say a prayer over yourself daily, so that God can help you beyond your carnal abilities.

There are three levels of the mind. These include:

#1 — The Conscious Mind

The conscious mind is thought activity that is operating on the surface level, present tense, "real time" (camera terminology) or cognitively. These are thoughts that you are more aware of and can access more readily, more quickly, and with more ease because you are processing them in your present tense functioning. These thoughts are usually thoughts that are associated with the task at hand and stay active in the forefront of the mind.

#2 — *The Subconscious Mind*

The subconscious mind is thought activity that is operating just below the surface level, in the past tense, in your memory, and has been downloaded from the conscious level mind after being practiced for about 30 days. These thoughts are not as readily or easily accessed without much personal evaluation. These thoughts are habit (habitual) on this level and usually serve as promoters or the actual justifiers of the conscious level thoughts.

For example, a wife may be angry with her spouse for not picking up his clothes from the floor, after asking him to do so several times. Her anger level rises and she can't stop thinking about it and even begins to watch for it. She thinks that the reason she becomes obsessed over this issue is because it is very important to her, and therefore she feels justified in her rising anger and obsession. However, the actual subconscious reason for her continued anger and obsessing is related to something else the husband did previously that offended her (such as a personal insult), which she has stored in her memory (intentional or not). At this point she has become critical of him and is watching for his faults.

This subconscious, unresolved offense from the insult makes the present clothes on the floor issue more serious. Therefore, the real anger at her husband is from the insult which is merely projected onto the clothes issue. Instead of letting the clothes issue be the perceived issue, the insult should be talked about and resolved as soon as possible. Otherwise, the clothes will continue to create a blow up, while the true issue remains hidden and unresolved.

The insult that she suppressed makes the clothes issue bigger and more personal to her. Because she does not realize cognitively that the insult is driving the intensity of the clothes issue, it will remain unresolved in her subconscious and continue to influence her conscious thoughts and emotional sensitivities.

#3 — The Unconscious Mind

The unconscious mind includes all experiences (especially the more emphasized ones) in the spirit, mind, emotions, or body (good or bad) that have been consistently repeated for more than six months and throughout your past. The longer you have been exposed and trained to do anything, then the more unconscious it is. It just integrates into the backdrop of your conscious and subconscious mind. The unconscious is what you think, say, or do without conscious pre-meditated thought at the time of the behavior and/or after the behavior has happened.

These experiences in the unconscious form a personal view of self, the world, and others. The unconscious serves as a "backdrop" for your view, perceptions, and life assumptions. The unconscious operates automatically and constantly. It is like a streaming video that never stops projecting its influence into your subconscious and conscious thought activity, emotions, spirit, and body.

The unconscious picture stays in place, while the subconscious thoughts are activated by periodic triggers and associations in the present tense. As I stated, the unconscious thoughts and behaviors function on a level that is a generalized backdrop of perceptions and experiences that are integrated into your personal world and self view. Your unconscious mind influences all of your surface (conscious) and below-the-surface (subconscious) perceptions.

Influence is the act or power of producing an effect without apparent force or direct authority, causing an effect in indirect or intangible ways, or to sway or have an effect on the condition or development. Here are two good examples:

Example #1 — Good son vs. bad son: A son who was raised by parents who practiced high morals and ethics themselves will positively construct that son's perceptions and assumptions as he gets older. Therefore, he will assume that it is normal to succeed in life and to develop relationships with people who empower his success (vs. hinder it). He will also think it is natural to develop compatible relationships.

Conversely, a son who was neglected, rejected, demeaned, and provoked by his parent(s) will develop a baseline assumption that he is not valuable and he will eventually act like it. He will pursue and develop sub-standard or destructive relationships and have anger, fear, insecurities, and low self-worth. This perception will become his reality because of his unconscious reference points. These building blocks constructed during his childhood and development years will download into his self-worth and image (esteem) and these will become the backdrop that influences his perceived worthiness. He may be an adult before he ever realizes that his low self-worth and self-image were learned and that he can change his future.

Example #2 — Good daughter gone bad: A daughter was raised by loving and moral role models. The daughter, while living in the home, never experienced traumas in her life and had every opportunity to develop and maximize her potential. Her parents may have taken great care in protecting her self-worth and self-image so that she would know her high value and worth in life.

However, the daughter, thinking that she is missing out on "fun" in life, becomes angry over her perceptions that she is being "treated like a child" and must no longer be "controlled" by her parents. The daughter, thinking she can "handle" or "control" any situation, puts herself into bad situations that will wound her and bring guilt and shame to her. She begins to self-inflict unnecessary wounds through multiple sex partners, drugs, alcohol, or other wounding behaviors. She is not only wounding herself, but her parents and those who love her also.

> **Self-inflicted wounds are unnecessary, and they hurt everyone, not just you.**

The shame and damage to her own worth and image becomes the backdrop that negatively influences her attractions to men. She no longer believes that she qualifies for a quality man (that would have been compatible to her previous healthy self-worth and image), so she does not associate with the good men with high morals. Instead she only qualifies for the bad ones who will readily tell her anything she wants to hear and "be" (temporarily) what he thinks will win her over. She has lowered her standard in men because she sees herself through her self-inflicted wounds, shame and self-disappointments.

What usually follows is the parents are forced to accept the lower quality guy so they will not lose their relationship with their daughter. All the while their hearts grieve for their daughter for whom they sacrificed to develop, love, and protect because they clearly understand what has happened to their daughter and they know the unnecessary hardships she will experience with that man who is not compatible to her potential.

She will then spend much energy and effort to be in denial about what she has done, even to the extent that she will defend his and her low moral standards, so that she will not have to face what she has done. When she comes to her senses at some point, she will attempt to improve the sub-standard husband or boyfriend but comes to a rude awakening that it's not possible to improve him (as she hoped), which will become a point of conflict with them on some level. The other possibility is that she will conform to his lower standards and bond with him in that way. The longer she stays with him and especially if she makes a marriage covenant with him, she will either have conflict with him or embrace his low morals and integrate into them so she can stay with him. This scenario develops even more if they have children together. If they are not married and have children, they still have to communicate with each other for the rest of their lives, unless one or both abandons the children.

Usually, the guilt perception that she is "abandoning" him and not keeping her word to him will prevent her from seeing past her emotional bond and keep her locked into him. It is usually not until the daughter has her own children, that she becomes more aware of her situation, because she wants her children to be healthy and have a family. Over time, the daughter, interestingly enough, taps into the principles that were instilled by her "controlling" parents, and she tries her best to teach her children well.

Hopefully her wound behaviors will be broken and the daughter will choose to become healthy again by repenting and restructuring her worth and image and once again think in terms of maximizing her potential and being in relationships with those who empower her to do so. This would be, of course, far better than the daughter consciously thinking that the substandard and immoral guy is compatible to her, and to compensate, she over focuses on all his positive traits. Sub-consciously or unconsciously she is in denial and represses the truth about this relationship and does not see the connection between her self-inflicted wounds and her negative attractions. In order to improve and become healthy, she must recognize the wounds, admit their effect on her, repent and denounce them, remove the wound behaviors (no longer practice them), and replace them with new productive thinking and behaviors that are in alignment with her God-given potential.

> Don't wait until you have a crisis to take action.

It's possible, but she will need to want it badly enough for it to happen, which will require that she experiences some eye-opening revelation of the truth. For some personalities, that eye opener, unfortunately, comes in the form of pain and suffering.

Thoughts produce corresponding behavior

Thoughts that are practiced will become beliefs and will become a normal part of your life. These normal thoughts will turn into corresponding behavior. This means that thoughts are like a seed that produces after its own kind.

Seeds do not produce fruit that is different than the nature of the seed. Corn seed will produce corn, wheat seed will produce wheat, and melon seed will produce melons, and so on. Seed planted inside of a woman produces a human, which is the fruit of that man and woman.

Like any seed and fruit, the soil and seed germinate (sprout the seed) and then matures (grows into a plant that will produce fruit for harvest). The seed of thought and the fruit of behavior is the same. It looks like this:

> Prolonged thought produces beliefs >
> produces behavior >
> produces habit and automatic behavior (maturity).

This is a law that governs all behavior just the same as the law of sowing seed and reaping fruit governs everything else on earth. You are a product of the seed that has been sown in your life by yourself or someone else.

I urge you to evaluate the fruit of your life and decide if it is good or bad and whether you have maximized every opportunity to produce good fruit in your life. You must maximize every opportunity, because in the finality of your physical life, your time to make the best of your life and have some eternal impact on others is very short. Make every change in yourself, beginning right now, in order to maximize your God-given potential.

Do not wait until you have a crisis to take action and be motivated. Too many people are crisis motivated. They wait until there is a crisis to be motivated to improve or change their life in specific areas.

If you are in crisis now, allow it to get your attention and inspire (or force) you to change. Do it today and do it now. Start somewhere and do not procrastinate. Do not listen to the voice of doubt and fear. Start small and build. Each positive result you have will be a stepping-stone to continue up that pathway. You will not do it perfectly so don't try to be perfect. It is okay to make mistakes, as long as you are putting forth your very best effort.

Pray and ask God to help you. He will do it. It does not matter what your denomination is or if you don't have one. God's love will make a way and will fulfill you and empower you. You will find out sooner or later that you will not always be adequate enough to overcome life's challenges in your own power. You need God. The sooner you accept that fact, the sooner you can experience life.

How patterns affect you

Recurring thoughts that are consistently practiced, whether true or false, truth or a lie, will become patterns of thought. This is truer if the thoughts are intentionally and intensely practiced. The thoughts that are more frequent and more intense will be established sooner and more deeply.

In fact the original thoughts and behavior that is trained to a child will become the bottom line reference points or default settings on that behavior. This is why it is crucial to train children in the way they should go in keeping with their particular giftings and bent (personality) so that when they are old they will not depart from that training (Proverbs 22:6 AMP).

The original training sets up the reference points for behavior. A reference point is an origination point that is necessary when surveying property so that you have a starting point to measure off the remaining measurements, boundaries, and shape of the property. Reference points are your starting points that give a basis from which to have exact definition, recognition and dimensions. This is one reason that early childhood wounds and traumas seem to define people as they get older. The early wound is the reference point to which they look for their identity and has influenced their boundaries and self-definitions.

> **You possess unique giftings and strengths. They are the real you!**

Both thoughts and physical action can become a "pattern." A pattern is a behavior or series of behaviors that are recurring, which are becoming or have become habit or character. Patterns of thought keep behavior patterns in motion. Periodic thoughts create and promote periodic behaviors. Webster's reveals that this word comes from a root word from which we get "paternal" or "father." It defines a pattern as: 1. "An ideal model" 2. Something used as a model for making things 3. Sample 4. An artistic design 5. Configuration.

When you are changing, you must change on purpose and by design. You must identify what you are changing, both in your thoughts and behavior, not just your behavior alone. If you try to change your behavior in any regard without changing the thoughts that create, promote, or justify that behavior, then you will have internal conflict and eventually return to that old behavior because thoughts create behavior.

When you are changing behavior as well as emotions, you must target the corresponding thoughts. Change your thoughts that support the behavior and you can change the emotions and behavior. For example, a girl who has been raised in a family that taught high morals for the first 18 years of her life will possess those standards as her baseline defaults. In fact, they are a part of her very heritage. If the daughter then violates those standards, she will have internal conflict. That conflict will cause misery that will result in depression, anger, confusion, or severe unpredictable mood swings.

Violations of values (spiritual and natural) is also a violation of self-respect and self-value, which will lower the way you see yourself and feel about yourself. Low self-value will lead to low perceived value from others. This also means you will seek acceptance from those with lower values as well.

This pattern is one of self-inflicted wounds that are unnecessary. You do not have to go out and violate yourself and your good relationships in order to find your identity. This will only bring you down and you will actually lose your real God-given core identity and create a false one that is dark, disappointed, depressed, angry, and destructive. Your true identity is found on a spiritual level in your God-given gifts and strengths.

They are the *real you*. They never go away, regardless of what you do good or bad. When you are ready, find out what they are, tap into them, and use them. They will work for you automatically and fulfill you the most.

Your giftings and strengths might be administration, hospitality, exhortation (encouraging), giving, leadership, organization, analyzing, or something else. You may not even be aware of the giftings and strengths that you have, but they are there, prompting you all the time. Your gifts are what you do automatically, most naturally, and they fulfill you the most and are your greatest propensities.

Gifts being automatic are different than learned behavior that has become automatic from practicing a behavior. Giftings are automatic, even if they have never been practiced. Your personal giftings are an "endowment" placed inside of you by almighty God.

What an amazing thought! God wanted to make you unique and fulfilled and empowered so that you could ultimately influence others eternally. Every person on earth has a different fingerprint. Likewise, you have unique gifts that are inside of you waiting and wanting to be used. Now you can develop your giftings so that you become more proficient in them and more familiar with them. This would be called "maximizing your potential" (see maximizing your potential section).

I encourage you to create new productive reference points in your life and resolve the old ones so that you can truly forget those things which are behind and maximize your God-given potential and purpose in life.

Chapter 4

The Law of Action

The Law of Action is a governing law of the physical realm. This is a law that applies to all physical behavior. As I explained in the Law of the Mind, when a behavior is practiced over a prolonged period of time, that behavior will eventually be conditioned, learned, and programmed as "normal" in the human spirit, emotions, mind, and body. Neurotransmitters fire in the direction of the behavior, which create neuro-pathways, which are highways (ruts in the brain) through which the behavior flows and is supported.

Your most frequently acted behavior on any given topic will download into the central nervous system and encode as "normal" because they are downloaded into files that are remembered. This muscle memory refers to frequent behavior that is remembered in your brain, mind, central nervous system, spirit, and body.

Each behavior has files and memory connected with it. This is how sophisticatedly created you are. Your brain remembers events, places, people, things, environments, and smells and makes associations. There is a part of your brain that stores emotional memory so that you can remember how something felt before. Your mind also remembers what you experienced, what you have done, how well you have done it, and all the related signals.

All of these memories are in files inside of you. Because you learned it, you can re-learn it or believe "you can't teach an old dog new tricks." The reason you can learn new things is because you are a learning being. If you understand God's laws (like gravity), then you can benefit from them. Just like planting new seed into the same old ground, you can experience new results in your life in a matter of weeks and months. Change of mind and behavior is the same.

How mental/physical behavior affects your spirit

Because we are learning beings, which have a mind and are human spirit beings, the mind and spirit of man also learns and is influenced by behavior. Behavior can be deposited down into the spirit and become the information that occupies the spirit in abundance. You then begin to speak with your words and act out in your physical body the very things that are in abundance in your spirit and mind.

This sheds some light on how our spiritual condition affects our mind and body and how our mental condition and what we do with our bodies affect our spiritual condition. They interface and work as a system.

Research shows that within approximately 10 minutes of introducing new thoughts or actions into your mind or expressions, neurological transmitters begin to transmit or "fire" in the direction of that behavior. In fact, your genes (gene expression) also express motion in the direction of your most frequently acted out behavior. This means that energy is being created in your brain and nervous system and even your body (muscle memory) to support, empower, or develop that behavior! The more it is practiced the more established it becomes. And again, after about 30 days the new behavior moves into the beginning stages of habit and after about six months the new behavior moves into the beginning stages of character.

Each time a behavior starts, the thoughts that promote that behavior also download to a deeper level, along with the physical behavior. Conscious thoughts download to the subconscious prior to the behavior moving into habit and into the unconscious prior to the behavior moving into character (automatic).

There is no clear research that establishes exactly how long the thoughts download from conscious to subconscious prior to those thought producing behaviors. However, I am of the opinion from my own counseling experience, that this time sequence depends upon the person's personality type. The outgoing personalities will turn thoughts into behavior much quicker than the reserved personalities, because reserved people typically will take more time processing the details so they can become more familiar with the behavior they will act out. The outgoing personalities usually implement a behavior more quickly because they are focused on results more than the details. However, once thoughts become actions, the thoughts and actions function on a corresponding level of conscious thoughts and conscious level behaviors.

Conscious thoughts/behavior are surface level and in the present tense, while subconscious thoughts/behavior occur just below the surface of conscious thought activity, support the conscious level activity, and serve as justifiers to the conscious level thoughts, beliefs, and behaviors.

For example, parents can consciously perceive that they are very angry at their child for spilled milk and feel justified in that extreme anger because of the spilled milk. But the real subconscious reason they are angrier than they should be with that type of minimal offense might be because they are still angry with their child from the day before. Maybe the child didn't clean up correctly, maybe some unrelated stressor is being projected into this issue, or maybe the parents are still "offended" over some other event.

Each behavior has files and memory connected with it.

The Law of Action is the expression of the physical body in an action or response. Every time there is physical motion, there are neurotransmitters that create neurological pathways through which the behavior will flow. Eventually internal "files" are established as a result of that behavior. It is necessary to provide more explanation of this process, so that you can be equipped to make desired changes and have the confidence that these behavior laws will work for you, and some understanding of how the process works:

How Activity-Dependent Stimulation Affects You

As I have already stated, neurological pathways are created in the brain and central nervous system because of neurotransmitters and synapses that are constructing these pathways as a result of the activity-dependent stimulation and learning that is occurring in the central nervous system and the entire nervous system. Information regarding the behavior is also collected by the nature of the behavior, which is encoded into programs that have files.

The central nervous system has memory (like small computer chips) that stores information and places it into files that are triggered and practiced (intentionally or not). This encoding in the mind and central nervous system is the premise of learned behavior. Imagine a massive filing cabinet where:

- Files consist of information that has been encoded into the human nervous system by practicing behavior.
- These files are logged in by subject matter.
- These files can be intentionally or unintentionally activated by thought activity that is occurring on the conscious, subconscious, or unconscious level.
- When activated, these files send the contents of the files into the brain, spinal cord, organs, muscles, and glands that can be felt in the nerves and body of the person.
- These files have information on all practiced behavior, including old expressions, wounds, pleasures, memories, subjects, experiences, etc.
- These files are triggered (activated) in the present tense by topics that are associated to that file.

These internal files contain the information that I have dissected into categories so that you can recognize when files that are on the inside of you have been activated. You can subsequently determine if they are positive files you want to reinforce or if they are old negative files you do not want to reinforce. Here are the 11 categories for the files within you:

File #1: Themes

In the case of these themes, which I also call "wound themes," they become files in the central nervous system and are encoded (like all practiced behaviors) and later are triggered by a topic in the present tense that is in some way associated with the theme.

A central theme that is related to a wound, sensitivity, or story line is that of being loved/not loved, worthy/not worthy, accepted/rejected, important/not important, etc. Themes have the same story line and reinforce the same messages and feelings regardless of the external stimuli (triggering person, place, thing, or topic).

It is a story line theme that plays in the brain, in the central nervous system, and is even felt inside the body. For example, a theme of not being loved will actually not allow people to fully accept love from others because they just cannot believe it, they doubt it, and their mind is always searching for a reason to invalidate the love that is being demonstrated to them.

Another reason they cannot totally accept love, or totally give love, is because they are afraid that giving and receiving love will require too much personal exposure. This exposure, they believe, will show they are inadequate in some way, which will then lead to rejection, which is their greatest fear.

File #2: Emotions

Emotions are corresponding feelings and accompanying emotions to the theme. For example, the feelings and emotions specifically associated with not being loved (along with other accompanying emotions and feelings) can be overwhelming and can create elevated stress, anxiety, and even panic.

People feel not loved in their central nervous system and in their body, and because the feelings are really there, the typical conclusion is that the not loved feelings are telling the truth. At that point, the feelings override the actual love that is being demonstrated from another person. When this happens, the person who does not feel loved will place such high demands and expectations on the other person (spouse, mother, father, etc.) that the gap, fault line, or void is impossible to fill with enough love. Consequently, when the love isn't sufficient to meet the impossibly high standards, then the unloved perception is further reinforced and the cycle continues.

The unloved feelings must be recognized as invalid for the very reason that the unloved feelings will continue regardless of the amount of love being shown. It's fake! The feelings come from a wound and theme in the story line.

> **Unloved feelings must be recognized as invalid.**

Sometimes the unloved feelings can be legitimate, such as when there really is a wound and a person is continuing to act out obvious behaviors that are hurting the unloved. For example, the husband who committed adultery and continues to tell his wife he does not love the other woman any more, yet the wife learns the husband is still seeing the other woman secretively. These messages are certainly not pretend and the feelings of not being loved are legitimate. These feelings can be magnified by an old previous adultery betrayal in an ex-husband or even in a father who was unfaithful and left his family.

File #3: Impulses

Impulses are a call to action or a prompting to act, move, or respond (physical, verbal, emotional, etc.), to do this or do that. It can also be an emotional reaction to something or someone that is not well thought out first. As the Scripture says, it is more effective to be slow to speak and swift to listen.

File #4: Emotional memory

Emotional memory is about how something was previously felt. It is a reproduction of the past emotions on a specific topic.

File #5: Internal messages

Internal messages are thoughts that speak to you and promote general/specific messages (obsessions, torment, fear, insecurities, peace, etc.) or promote mental activity that speaks to you inside your head ("They don't like you" or "You're not important" or "You can't do this" or "It is better to not try than to fail" or "You can do this" or "Have faith in God" or "You are too vulnerable so keep your walls up").

If the messages are specifically saying you are not loved, then you will have doubts. Internal messages like, "Look at the way your spouse hugged you, he/she doesn't really love you" or "You are not that important to that person" or "Be afraid of intimacy and closeness" or "Don't open up that much" or "They are probably thinking about their old girlfriend/ex-spouse and not you" can turn into mental obsessions that will not stop. They will come frequently or they can be periodic, and these thoughts can turn into "torment." In some more severe cases, these thoughts can develop into paranoia or even a personality disorder.

File #6: Brain associations

An association is a related or similar experience that reminds you or takes your mind to the same or similar experience. For example, a beautiful lake may remind you of the lake in front of your hotel room on your honeymoon and the good or bad experiences you had. An intersection may remind you of a traffic accident, a disappointment may remind you of all your failures, a rejection may remind you of your loneliness and other people who have rejected you and the feeling it created inside of you.

File #7: Muscle memory

Muscle memory is a conditioned somatic (bodily) position, symptom, and motion. This takes the form of flight, fight, tensions, anxiety, stomach nausea, blood pressure, sitting up, facial expressions, tone of voice, hand or foot or arm motions, movements, riding a bicycle, reflexes, muscle tension, programmed sensations, etc. It was reported in the Vietnam War that some deceased soldiers lying in transport helicopters in body bags would sit up even though they were no longer alive. This is an example of the energy, impulses, and muscle memory still being activated based upon programmed behavior.

File #8: Mental-picture memory

Memories are past experiences that are stored and recalled (physical, emotional, etc.) in your mind. These experiences then serve as reference points. [Note: the most effective way to look into the subconscious (just below the surface) into your thoughts, emotions, behavior, and even motives is to look in your memory.]

The data in your memory is already stored, and all you have to do is go into that "room" and extract that information. For example, if you have a traumatic memory of not being or feeling loved (real or perceived), then you may actually feel uncomfortable with being loved even if being loved is the very thing you desire the most. However, you can create a new memory (reference point) by loving and receiving love. Every time you have a new positive experience, it is a building block for your new reference point to which you can refer.

Looking back in your memory for the sole purpose of reinforcing your bad experience will cause you to live in the past and to "bond" with the past. This is called "trauma bonding" (see Trauma Bonding section) and will make you unfit and unhealthy.

File #9: Triggers

Triggers are actually "brain associations." The brain associates a present tense stimuli with the past experience which created pain and is similar in some way to the past painful experience. These associations can be topics, people, events, colors, smells, environments, pain, words, scenarios, places, sounds or anything else that reminds you of your past trauma, wound, or painful experience. I would like to remind you that the experience doesn't have to be logically painful to someone else, what matters is how it affected you.

Clinically, when you experience pain, you remember relative to the level or intensity of pain it caused. So the more painful, the more it impacts your memory and it creates a "reference point" in your memory. But additionally, that reference point is like a wound that takes time and intentional effort to heal. From the time that the wound takes place to the time it heals, and sometimes long after that, there is "energy" that builds up around that wound because of the impact it had and because of the energy and time to either manage it or to heal it. The more attention you pay to something, the more energy is built up around it.

This is created by neurotransmitters that attach to neurons that have energy in them and fire around the area where a wound takes place and has pain and behaviors around it called "wound behaviors." The longer you take to heal, the stronger the wound gets and the more time it will take to dismantle it which gives fears that develop from it more time to solidify and "infect" the belief system.

> **Do not look into your past to reinforce a bad experience.**

I use the word *infect*, because fears work their way into your beliefs and convince you that they are telling the "truth." When you believe that fear messages are true, then they become more powerful in you, more frequent, and you eventually "obey" their promptings. Fears also establish comfort zones around themselves so that you experience discomfort when you violate the fear's rules. You must become cognitively aware of these fear messages (which come up from the subconscious and unconscious mind), so that you can notice them when they speak to you. This is essential in intervening into them and breaking their power over you.

When you do this, you will be uncomfortable for a while until you intentionally replace the fear behaviors with new healthy ways of thinking and acting. Then you must practice the healthy ways until they become the new norm, even if you are uncomfortable in the meantime. At this point you will be comfortable outside of the fears and comfortable in your new healthy way of living. I therefore, strongly encourage you to identify your old wounds and deal with them immediately.

File #10: Self-image and self-worth perceptions

Self-worth determines how you value yourself and how you perceive value from other people. It also involves what you think you are worthy of or what you qualify for in relationships, potential, success or in good things happening to you. This also includes your responses/reactions to these perceptions.

Self-image determines how you see/view yourself and how you perceive that you are seen by others, which also includes the amount of recognition you need to feel good. Image management gets involved in self-image, which involves the demonstration of certain behaviors that you learned will impress people or cause them to accept you more readily. Some people lose themselves in this so deeply that they are not authentic and they spend most or all of their time managing and protecting their image; that becomes their identity upon which their confidence is based. Consequently, they develop a fear of exposure and vulnerability to people seeing through their facade and seeing their wounds and insecurities. This is a miserable and tormenting existence.

Some sons and daughters in healthy homes (where the parents did a good job raising their children) will once in awhile, when they are around 16 years of age, get a sense that they missed out on something or lost some freedom. Through peer pressure, they hear about what they have "missed out on," and whether it's real or perceived, the children still think they have missed out. They begin to rebel while they still live at home or they wait until they move out or go to college. Once they are "free," they go on a destructive pathway and wound themselves unnecessarily.

One such person was David. He grew up in an affluent home in the mid-west where there were moral principles to follow, he was not abused or neglected, and his parents stayed married. In fact, his parents did things right. David was trained to be confident and feel good about himself. He also had an assertive and independent personality that served as a destructive mechanism when it was misused. He began to feel he was being treated like a child, so he decided to go looking for adventure. He found it! You can wound yourself very quickly, you know.

Often, young adults who have been well trained think they can "handle" most people and most bad situations. They are strong, but think they are stronger than they really are.

In addition, if they feel they have missed something, that always ends destructively. In these situations, the good girls go after the "bad boys" who really don't want help and who are destructive and the good boys go after the "bad girls" who are starved for love and who are willing to do almost anything to feel valued. The healthy chase the unhealthy.

David, healthy and strong, went after a wounded girl and he desired her improvement more than she desired it for herself. Remember this principle: YOU CANNOT WANT AND PURSUE SOMEONE ELSE'S IMPROVEMENT MORE THAN THEY DO FOR THEMSELVES. If you try, you will fail miserably and it will create failure, feelings of not being good enough, co-dependency, rejection, feeling misunderstood, and being blamed in the end. David wanted the girls to get better more than they wanted it, and this locked him into changing them. At this point, his own self-worth was at stake, for if they didn't change, he didn't feel good about himself, and that in turn lowered his own self-image even more.

He started out strong, but after all his sexual and emotional wounds, which included a secret abortion for one of his girlfriends, he was afraid and ashamed, and now he had to deal with a secret past that was affecting his self-confidence.

Without question, David was stuck in guilt. He began to believe that no healthy girl would want him if his private sexual past were known. In order to push away his self-disappointment and shame, he blamed his parents for controlling him. That way it wasn't his fault. He was, of course, ashamed to tell them what he had done, so he kept it inside and tried to just ignore it. He developed a mixture of anger and hatred for his parents, even though he was the one damaging himself. From a good home and a church upbringing, he rebelled against it all.

He eventually moved to another state and married a woman who was totally incompatible. It seemed glamorous at first, but it became a very hard road later. They unexpectedly had a child before marriage and because of it, he feared that he could not support the child. He also wondered what kind of woman he had embraced and taken on to be his child's mother! She was certainly not mature enough to be a mother, which is most often the case.

This scenario left David dependent on his parents to help with the child because the child's mother didn't have a good enough relationship with her parents. When David finally reached out to his parents, they refused to help and told him that he had to find his own way to solve the problems that he had created for himself. The parents were ashamed and embarrassed, but they eventually did reach out and help after they got over the initial shock.

Sometimes in this situation, a new and frightened young mother will make the father of the child sign away his rights to the child, thinking this creates a healthier environment. In reality, what always ends up happening is that when the child reaches a certain age, knowing the biological father becomes the focus ... and resenting the mother who kept everyone separated is the natural end result.

This was not the case with David and his wife, Kathy. They eventually were married and he got a minimum-wage job and she worked part time. They had another child and life was very stressful in their small apartment as they tried to live together, work, and juggle the children. For a while this worked, but eventually he began to resent her. It really wasn't her fault that she was incapable of doing more than she was doing.

David was able to get better jobs which gave them more income, but Kathy couldn't seem to get rid of her poverty mentality and low self-worth. She grew up that way and such things cannot be quickly restructured just because you get married and have children. In truth, demands of marriage and parenting can cause your insecurities and immatureness to come out even more!

David tried to help Kathy be a better mother and wife (because he had good role models), but he began to be critical of her and show non-acceptance. As his anger and resentment increased, this led to even more strife and conflict in the home. Subconsciously, David was trying to turn Kathy into the type of woman that his mother was.

Kathy did love David, but she began to disrespect him out of her own immaturity and hatred that stemmed from the fact that he was not accepting her. Disappointment set it. They couldn't seem to get ahead in their relationship, though they both tried hard to make it work. Interestingly, everything he had rebelled against with his parents ... became the very things that he was trying so hard to get back into his own home! What he used to hate about his "controlling" parents became his goal. He even tried getting Kathy to go to church, which only created more feelings of rejection and frustration for her. When she would go to church with him, she showed no interest. She didn't grow up knowing God, much less wanting Him.

His effort to lead in this area, something that was important to him because it impacted his own life and the lives of their children, fell on deaf ears. She wasn't following him, and this caused even deeper damage to their relationship.

They battled on, and years later, something happened that pushed David over the edge. He came into my office in tears. He was confused, for together they were making $80,000 a year, a great success for them, and he wanted to buy a new home that cost only $60,000. Though they easily qualified for the loan, Kathy refused.

She was afraid and angry. It turns out that Kathy felt uncomfortable in a new home. It went against everything inside of her. She felt more comfortable in an old run-down house and she had no vision and no experience beyond that.

It was at this point that David realized afresh and anew that his choices were keeping him bound. Kathy was stuck in a "poverty mentality." She had grown up with little or nothing and did not have a role model to show her how to develop her potential and succeed in life. And now ... he was stuck as well. Having a family with a woman who had a poverty mentality and low self-worth was keeping them both in bondage. He had not succeeded in changing her, like he once thought he was capable of doing. He thought he could change her and that she would love him and that she would sacrifice enough to make him accept her like she was. This was a scary and almost hopeless place for both of them.

David cried a lot that day, but agreed with me that he would not leave her or his family. Then he and Kathy came in together for help. In therapy, we worked on both of them until they began to see themselves differently. I helped them to understand and develop their potential as a couple. I also retrained her in the areas of her self-worth and self-image that she did not receive when she was growing up. It was a long hard road that got easier as they grew together.

I also encouraged Kathy to stay married to David and keep their family together and to think in terms of sowing and reaping. We typically hear about sowing and reaping in a negative light, but it is also very positive and is the guaranteed way to get planned results. I told her, "It takes about six to nine months for a crop to come up after planting it. It always works that way. It's a law of God and His universe. You can't escape it, so decide where you and your husband want to be in six to nine months and in five years. Then together, design a plan, write it out, and make it clear. Walk out the plan and modify as needed as you go. Plant the seeds, water them, and stay your course." They embraced this principle together and they both began to prosper and develop.

A significant part of Kathy's development and transformation was related to her self-worth and self-image. Until she felt worthy, she didn't think she qualified for a better life, and until her self-image was re-constructed, she wrongly perceived how she viewed David as a man and herself as a woman.

In addition, I helped David forgive his parents for the true and perceived wrongs they had done to him. His previous anger and hatred for his parents, and for himself, was washed away. He and his parents eventually developed a good relationship. Kathy also forgave herself for the things she had done and soon she too was reconciled with her father and mother.

It was then that Kathy accepted her husband on a whole new level. Not only did he see her differently, but she was beginning to value herself more as well. How you view yourself is how you believe other's see you. This case turned out to have a good ending, but unfortunately it is the exception instead of the rule. If you are in a similar scenario, don't be ashamed to reach out for help.

File #11: Feelings, bodily sensations, and cravings

This last file includes feelings, bodily sensations, and cravings. I remind you that the encoding in these files occurs whether the behavior is productive/destructive, wrong/right, good/bad, or negative/positive. Even if there is a break in the behavior, it can still be a pattern of behavior. This is because a pattern doesn't have to be "constant" behavior, but the pattern is consistent.

There is a difference between consistent and constant behavior. A pattern may be only periodically destructive, but can still be a pattern. For example, a man can get drunk only on weekends and develop a pattern in doing so. This pattern would be consistent, but he does not constantly get drunk. However, the pattern is still stored and will be activated at the programmed time. If the man, for some reason, does not get drunk for a weekend or several weekends, his mind, body, and nerves will remind and prompt him with impulses, associations, cravings, and memories that he is programmed to do so and he can be driven and even tormented until he gets drunk again. In fact, he may have to obey those cravings so that the torment and anxiousness (maybe even anxiety) will subside. Of course this type of self-medicating can lead to alcoholism.

HOW BEHAVIORAL SEQUENCE AFFECTS YOU

When a person experiences something from an external source (television, radio, another person, scenery, sounds, touch, contact, kiss, slap, etc) or from an internal source (present tense thoughts, emotions, memories, temptations, sensations, feelings, hurt, anger, offenses), whether pleasure or pain, there is a sequence of responses that occur. It goes like this:

> The stimuli (external and internal) >
> receptor (processing in the mind) >

access beliefs >
access references points >
access beliefs >
decision made >
signals sent to the brain, spinal cord, organs, and body >
files on that behavior activated >
muscles, glands, and emotions activated >
response of movement and behavior >
observation of the interaction and experience >
processed if wrong or right, good or bad >
acceptance or rejection.

Basically this diagram shows that stimuli of any kind can affect your whole system if you practice, embrace, obey, validate, accept, or believe it.

Why access/entry points are so important

External incoming stimuli in the form of information, a substance, a person, influences, words, images, sounds, smells, or power source, can enter into the spirit, mind, emotions, or body through your entry and access points.

Here are six entry and access points to consider:

Point #1: Eyes

Your eyes are the windows of the soul. "Your eye is the lamp of the body…if your eye is sound then your body is full of light," says Matthew 6:22 (AMP).

I have often looked into the eyes of clients and others and very quickly saw fear, anger, insecurity, low self-worth, seduction, deception, shame, secrecy, darkness, death, life, joy, and more. This is why I often have couples or families who are healing and resolving issues look into each other's eyes. This will not only create spiritual and emotional intimacy, but it will connect them in their agreement to resolve and experience closure to a problem.

Point #2: Mouth

Spoken words are a reflection of what is on the inside of your heart, mind, emotions, body, self-image, self-worth, etc. That is why it is said that death and life are in the power of the tongue.

Point #3: Ears

What you hear, especially what you purposefully subject yourself to, will enter all three levels of your mind and eventually your spirit. Be careful what you hear because it multiplies inside of you.

You are the first one to hear what you are saying. Say what you want and say it as a planned confession on a daily basis so that you can hear it. You can reset your mindset by determining what you hear. If you hear death and depression, then death and depression will become a part of your thinking and emotional state and eventually your behavior in some regard.

On the other hand, if you hear life and purpose, then life and purpose will become a part of you.

Point #4: Touch

Human touch is powerful. It connects people and is a form of affection. Physical touch is a key element used in prayer, massage therapy, physical therapy, assaults, balancing, facial identification for visually impaired, handshakes, and more.

Point #5: Recurring behavior

Strip yourself of anything that resembles your former way of living and be constantly renewed. Wisdom is the principle thing, and relationships either bless or curse.

Point #6: Wounds

A wound that stays unhealed (unresolved) becomes an entry point for emotional infection and worsening states of mind and being. Left unresolved, emotions such as hate, rejection, bitterness, unforgiveness, and even murder can be developed. It is like an emotional infection that invades the soul and eventually the spirit.

Likewise, a physical wound that is unhealed attracts parasites. Don't you find it interesting that parasites know that a wound is still open and unresolved in the physical body?

When you experience an emotional, mental, or physical trauma or hurt that wounds you, it is imperative that as soon as possible you forgive, let go, and receive healing over that wounding experience. Even if no one else thinks that you should be wounded in the first place, get healed.

Wounds affect different people differently. If two soldiers are standing near each other and both are hit by the same mortar round, they will each be wounded a little differently, feel it differently, and recall it differently. Sometimes one will be injured and the nearby person not wounded at all.

Your experiences that wounded you are valid because you were wounded. Therefore, you must not ignore the wound or obey the embarrassment of having to admit you were wounded and in need of healing.

Once you become aware that you have been wounded, you should have one objective only and that is to address it and be healed as soon as possible. Do not allow the fact that you have a "right" to stay wounded keep you in that wounded state!

> **Wounds affect different people differently.**

Validate the wound by getting it healed in every way possible. One simple way to know that you are healed is that you can expose the wound and talk about it without the same or similar pain. After you are healed, it may be uncomfortable to openly discuss it, but you are no longer afraid of it.

An unresolved/unhealed wound is an access point for infection and for spiritual influences to "oppress" or "possess" a person eventually. The basic definition from *Webster's* of a tomb is: "a vault, chamber or grave for the dead."

With something that is dead, there is always a good or bad memory. A wound is a place of memory as well. As a result of a wound, there is often the death or loss of a relationship, dream, aspiration, or even a person's life.

It is also important for me to bring to your attention that spiritual forces, which are evil in nature, often reside in tombs. A tomb is a place where people have been buried (death), a place of a negative memory, and a place where there is an opening in the ground or building with doors and access points (chamber).

Listen to this:

- And as soon as He got out of the boat, there met Him OUT OF THE TOMBS a man [under the power] of an unclean spirit." (Mark 5:2)
- This man continually lived in the tombs…." (Mark 5:3)
- Night and day among the tombs and on the mountains he was always shrieking and screaming…." (Mark 5:5)
- And they came to Jesus and looked intently and searchingly at the man who had been a demoniac, sitting there, clothed and in his right mind…." (Mark 5:15)

My point is to reveal the spiritual truth about emotional wounds. If they stay unresolved, eventually they attract the Kingdom of darkness, which may include demonic spirit beings that can oppress and torment your soul. This is much like an open flesh wound that, when it stays unresolved and unhealed, will eventually attract micro-organisms that will infect the open wound.

You can be healed! You are not the exception that represents the only one in the population who cannot be healed.

You cannot be free and healed by isolating yourself in fear and shame from the wounds of the past and present. Admit the wounds in you and be willing to reach out to qualified people who can actually help you, both naturally and spiritually. Remember, do not neglect the spiritual part of you which is actually the real and core you. I often tell my clients that a wound, crisis, or trauma will either cause you to get closer to God or to get further away from Him. If you run to Him, He will help you heal. If you run away from Him, He cannot help you heal. God comes in by invitation, not always by necessity.

This analogy should not be scary or a mystery, but rather a warning that wounds should be healed and resolved as soon as possible. Additionally, I will not attempt to make a theological stand by sharing these insights with you. As a Therapist, I have to help people on a mental, emotional, physical, and spiritual level. You have to address all of these areas of the human system in order to accomplish healing and wholeness. Therefore the spirit realm, which is just as real as the physical realm, must be dealt with and not ignored. This is true regardless of your spiritual or religious background, or lack of it. There comes a time that you have to address all areas of your life if you really want to be free and whole.

> **All areas of your life need to be addressed if you want to be whole and healthy.**

Remember, wound behaviors always develop during the time of a wound. A wound behavior can be acted out if the wound is either unhealed or healed. This serves as a deception to many people because they believe that a healed wound means there are no wound behaviors. A wound behavior can be present and often is, after the wound and hurt is healed. You have to examine yourself for a wound as well as wound behaviors.

Also remember that one obvious sign of a wound is hypersensitivity to certain topics and themes. People often refer to these as buttons as in "he pushes my buttons."

The sign of a healed wound, but the presence of wound behavior, is over-compensation and over-response. This is when people experience small offenses and respond with high intensity. This is usually because the small violation reminds them, on some level and in some way, of the old or fresh wound, and they are responding to the wound and not to the present minor issue.

Healing is for you. If not now, then when?

SECTION III

DEALING WITH YOUR PAST

Dealing with your past requires that you examine your past, not for the purpose of reliving the pain and self-condemnation, but to make sure that you have forgiven (God, self, and others), and that you are not repeating the same behaviors or emotions or relationships. God created your memory for a reason, and it was to use it not to be afraid of it and avoid or deny it. If you have hurts and wounds from your past, then they are not resolved until you identify, forgive, say you forgive, and actually experience the emotional pain.

The evidence that your past is resolved will be confirmed by the absence of the same pain when you think and talk about your past. If you can talk about your past, then you are free. If you cannot, you may not be totally free. Talking about your past with just anyone is usually not wise, so I'm not suggesting talking to anyone. However, at the appropriate time and with the appropriate person, you must be able to. If you cannot, then you must deal with your past.

Chapter 5

Resolving Your Past

Resolving the past is so important that John 4 records that Jesus spent several hours one day with a Samaritan woman (the woman at the well) resolving her past. Afterwards, she told everyone that He told her everything she had ever done (her past). In John 4:39-42, others came to hear Jesus for themselves because of this woman's testimony.

That message is one of the central themes here. You must address the past, confront it, and resolve it before you can be healed and move on. This is also necessary in order to reach your full potential. In this book, I explain in detail how to resolve the past and change your life to the extent that you can walk in health in your spirit, soul, and body.

Wounds are a Part of Life

We all experience or have experienced some kind of past hurt, wound, or trauma on a single or recurring basis. That's life! Those past hurts and wounds will be resolved by design or be emotionally suppressed and/or mentally repressed and therefore remain internally intact on some level.

Wounds are often suppressed so that we can continue to function after the wound, around the wound, or from the wound. The suppression usually occurs under the pretense or wishful thinking that "time heals everything." The fact is that all past experiences (good and bad) integrate on some level into our self-worth and/or self-image as we develop from childhood through the teenage years to adulthood. The self-worth and self-image then project forward into the present tense behavior throughout our adulthood.

Past hurts, wounds, and traumas (i.e. rapes, murders, divorces, molestations, failures, lost opportunities, abuse, etc.) influence our perceptions, decisions, actions, responses, and overall attitudes. These past negative experiences especially reveal themselves during times of stress.

For example, imagine a small fracture in a water pipe that is not detected when the water pressure is low or moderate. But when the pressure is turned up, the fracture cannot keep the water inside and the water sprays out, sometimes uncontrollably, until the pressure goes back down.

When this happens with people, it's always a sign of unresolved wounds. Any time there is a recurring overresponse or overcompensations in behavior, then you can consider it a fact that there is an unresolved wound attached that is driving the behavior.

WAITING TO BOIL!

Like carrying a suitcase around, people carry their unresolved wounds, hurts, and emotions around with them, while at the same time they falsely believe that they are not doing it. Of course we know, and certainly the spouse knows, that the unresolved past is manifesting itself into the present tense behavior. This is evidenced by the way people respond to a minor offense with a major reaction. Something triggered them.

"Triggers" are a topic, theme, conflict, scenario, person, environment, or smell that reminds us of a past wound or violation. We may not cognitively recognize the association at the time, but the past is indeed associated with our present response.

Clinically, the mind interacts with the central nervous system, which in turn pulls up its files on the topic. The old programs run, and that always includes some kind of response. If the wound is unhealed or the old program is still alive and has not been dismantled, then the overresponse will not match the perceived violation.

For example, a husband can have a job that the wife knows requires him to work some overtime. He usually comes home at 6 p.m., but tonight he arrives home at 7 p.m. When he walks in the door, even though he telephoned her to say he would be late, she begins to overrespond with anger, sarcasm, or hurt that he was not home and that she was alone for that time and may even go so far as to say he "lies" to her and does not love her, that if he loved her he would be home at the same time every day, or that the job is more important than his family. As she says these things, she is on a topic that emotionally escalates into a high level response to his low level violation.

> Do old wounds still trigger a response in you?

What has happened is that her husband coming home late reminded her on a subconscious or unconscious level of her absentee father, who was not present a lot because of work when she was growing up, or of her father who abandoned her through divorce, or of her father who had not been interested in his family for years. Her old wounds and the programs that are birthed from them were triggered and she acted it out on her husband. It took her further than she wanted to go, went too deep, and stayed there too long. Unfortunately this scene will be acted out numerous times in her life, even though she may try to stop it or suppress it, until she confronts the wound, forgives her father (if she hasn't already), and experiences healing.

HEALING IS REQUIRED

Regardless of the nature of the destructive behavior, there must eventually be a healing and restoration process. This process requires that all past wounds, sins, mistakes, faults, and offenses be identified, confessed, and forgiven in order for healing and restoration to begin.

At this point the healing and restoration process can begin and, in most cases, the confession and forgiveness does start the healing process. The healing has just started and must be completed before the old behavior will be gone, replaced by a new one that is automatic and part of the normal behavior and identity. At that point, a person can experience wholeness.

Healing is when each part is well and wholeness is when all of the healed parts are working together as a whole system.

The initial healing process will allow a wound and the pain associated with it to be released. It is like an infected wound that is finally drained, cleaned out, sown up, and healed to the extent that it can be subjected to stress or an impact without the same pain as before. That is why a sign of healing is when you can address or expose a previously painful issue and no longer experience that pain. Sure, the same external trigger or reminder can still be present, but it will not have the ability to create pain in you because the old wound is healed. The old issues that were once painful and scary won't possess the same hypersensitivities either.

> Healed behavior practiced over time will become the new norm.

Additionally, after the healed behavior is practiced over time, it will download as normal and consequently the same issues will not have the same effect in your central nervous system or even your body. The reason for this is that the old neurological pathways that were created by the old wound behaviors are no longer open and active. This means that you can remember the past without experiencing the pain of the past.

But remember, this is only accomplished by completing the entire process of confession, forgiveness, healing, and replacing the old with the new behaviors until the new behaviors are automatic.

This is a purposeful process that does not happen just because time passes or because you feel better. Your feelings must conform to your decisions. And if you cannot complete the change alone, find someone qualified who can help you. There is no shame in being helped. Finding help if you need it is actually wisdom.

Resolved vs. Suppressed

Eventually these past wounds either get resolved or further suppressed. When resolved and healed, the memory of the event will still be there to some extent, but the trauma and pain from that event will not be actively felt or re-lived if remembered. It may even be an unpleasant memory, but not have the associated pain or trauma.

Many clients tell me during sessions that they can't, or do not want to, remember the past. This is usually because they do not want to remember and don't want to feel the pain. They are afraid that if they remember they will feel the shame, guilt, and related emotions. In most cases this simply means that this past memory of the wound has been repressed and the pain suppressed.

As I stated before, it may be forgiven but not healed. When a memory is repressed it is curbed, subdued, restrained, and excluded from consciousness. When something is suppressed it is put down (stuffed down) by force, subdued, and kept from being known. Feelings, personality, wounds, enjoyment, laughter, acceptance, gifts, talents, emotions, hurts, pains, or even potential can be suppressed. Suppressed usually relates to emotions and repressed relates to memories.

Resolving the past is a purposeful act that requires action, not avoidance and denial. Resolving requires that you confront your past and admit that the past exists and that it mattered. You cannot say, "I don't want to talk about it," and at the same time resolve it. Those who ignore or avoid are hopeful that it will go away or that everyone, including themselves, will forget it. Time just makes things worse.

People who do this have convinced themselves that it is easier to blame their destructive behaviors on someone or something else rather than accept that there is something inside of them that needs repair. They don't realize that the destructive behaviors are coming from within.

The exception to this rule is when you are in a relationship with a person who is legitimately destructive, neglectful, or abusive. If you are not married, and especially if you have no children, and you are in a destructive relationship, then you must get out of that relationship even if you think you are abandoning that person. You must realize that you do not have the authority or the power to change that person. You can't force it. Furthermore, your love or sacrifices will never be enough to change that person.

Many people believe they are the exception to all the other people who tried and failed to change someone. They think on some level that their love will be strong enough to penetrate the problems, but they will come to a rude awakening that their love is not being appreciated like they think.

> You cannot change someone else if that person refuses to change. It's simply impossible!

Listen, your love, even though sincere, cannot change someone who is incapable, unreliable, insincere, or any combination of these three. If you continue in a destructive relationship, the only one who will change is you, and it will be for the worse. You are not the "Savior." There is only one Savior and you are not Him and you will never take His place. You can lead a person to the Savior, but you can never be that person's Savior.

I encourage you to resign from that perceived position right now. A relationship was never intended by God to minimize your potential and destroy you. I know that it is very hard to try to convince you of the truth when your self-worth is already low. That low worth will tell you that it does not matter if you are damaged by that bad relationship because you don't value yourself anyway.

The unfortunate truth is that people do what they subconsciously think they deserve. This is really an issue of self-worth that needs reconstructing and brought into alignment with God's view and value that He places on you. Genesis 1:27 says that God created us, male and female, in His own image and likeness. You are created with an image that originated from the creator of all the heavens and earth, and that great value is placed on you is evidenced by the fact that you exist and by what happened on the Cross. It does not matter what church background you have or if you have no church background at all. You are still valued by God.

Let me ask you, how would you act if you had the slightest thought that I could be telling you the truth and that your low self-worth was not telling you the truth? You have nothing to lose if I am wrong and much to gain if I am right.

Therefore, seek out God's love, because He is love and that love will help you and will put life into you. This kind of love will resolve the past, low self-worth, all fears, all sins, failures, shortcomings, mistakes, and horrible decisions.

I am not talking about a denomination, religion, or ceremony. I am talking about the love of God for you that you can allow into you right now. It is impossible to get hurt by God's love. You have taken risks in many other ways without much regard for yourself, so take this risk. You don't even have to deserve it.

Now, let's talk about suppressed emotions. This means that an emotion is targeted in an attempt to not feel that emotion again (at all or in that same way). It also means to put down by force and to keep from being known (by self or another person looking in).

If you want to settle and resolve a negative emotion, instead of suppressing it, and you try to do it by ignoring or avoiding the negative emotion, then the emotion will continue because the hurt or wound behind the experience was not resolved. You have to address the wound experience and the thoughts that produce those unwanted emotions. Only targeting the negative emotions will do you no good. They will remain internally active.

For example, when people display immediate rage at an injustice of some kind, the rage is connected to their own injustice they suffered. In a way they are responding as if they were protecting or rescuing themselves when the wound happened or they are acting out rage on their perpetrator from the past each time they see a present injustice. In most cases, however, the suppressed emotions are stuffed inside, along with the associated memory, and they have no idea where those emotions originated.

The suppressed emotions are usually internalized and masked under excuses and transference to other people. Guilt motivation, blame, and anger are also common techniques that are used (intentionally or not) to mask and hide unresolved wounds. The wounds are also enabled to remain and are therefore internalized and pushed down deeper by the false assumption or belief that "time heals all."

Some common avoidance statements come forth in the form of the following statements:

"Let's get past it."
"I was not angry ... I was only frustrated."
"That does not bother me anymore."
"That did not bother me that much."
"I don't think about that anymore."
"That happened a long time ago."
"I forgot about that a long time ago."
"I don't know ... I can't remember."
"If you wouldn't push my buttons ..."

These statements are common avoidances, excuses, denials, and fears that continue to suppress the real effects of past wounds. I will continue throughout this book to explain and reveal the extent of the influence on behavior that is created by unresolved past wounds.

Repressed memories become apparent when a person can't remember a past experience but their memory range should be able to recall the information during a particular time period, or when the memory is fragmented and only pieces can be recalled and questions about the past remain. This is similar to the memory of a person who has had a traumatic traffic accident and their memory for some time period before and after the accident cannot be recalled. Victims of molestation often cannot remember details of the event.

Repressed means to curb, subdue, or to exclude from consciousness, and you cannot reach your full potential if you repress or suppress your emotions.

Forgiveness vs. Healing

Clients often tell me that they are forgiven for their past and therefore they do not need to "go back there" and deal with it anymore.

My response is, "You may be forgiven, but are you healed?"

There is a distinct difference between forgiveness and healing. Even though forgiveness is the first part of healing, forgiveness requires a separate act. For example, a person can break another person's leg and ask forgiveness and receive it. However, the wounded person's leg still has to go through the healing process, even though forgiveness has occurred.

I also ask, "Are you still acting out wound behaviors as a result of the wound?"

During the time that the broken leg is healing, the behavior of that person will be modified to accommodate the weakness, sensitivities, and pain. In order to function while it is healing, they may have to limp, walk slower, etc., as we have already discussed. They will also remember the pain, and may walk or run differently for the rest of their life.

After the leg is actually healed and strong again (which is a process), they may continue to act out these negative and destructive wound behaviors unintentionally. They are not healed or restored and therefore are not retrained.

You may be forgiven, but are you healed?

Most people who do this never "connect the dots" from the present wound behavior to the past wound. Some do see a connection, but don't know what to do about it. They often try to stuff down the unresolved past and cover their unhealed wounds.

There are some who actually go through the forgiveness and healing process but are still acting out the wound behaviors. This keeps them trapped in the past with their behaviors, not able to totally be free and separated from the past.

After forgiveness and healing, the wound behaviors must be identified, denounced, removed, and replaced with new healthy behaviors that replace the old ones. This replacement behavior must be based upon the productive difference between the old and the new. For example, the liar must tell the truth. The thief must give and pay retribution in numerous ways. It may not be possible to completely replace what was stolen, but some of the damage can be repaid, even if they stay anonymous. The judgmental and critical people must begin to love and have mercy. The withdrawn and shy must begin to meet people and place themselves in situations where they must develop confidence. This can be done in a safe enough way while they are developing their confidence. Replacement of the old is absolutely necessary in order to complete the change.

Forgiving self or someone else requires a decision to forgive from the mind and heart with sincerity and not rehash the offense. Healing requires:

- That the wound be identified.
- That the wound be labeled correctly.
- That you acknowledge that it mattered.
- That you confess it.
- That you let it go to God.

I believe a person cannot be healed deeply enough unless they involve God in the process through prayer and confession. I Peter 5:7 (AMP) says to cast all cares, anxieties, worries, and concerns once and for all on Him (God) because He cares about you affectionately and watchfully. James 5:16 (AMP) says to confess your faults one to another so that you may be healed and restored to a spiritual tone of mind and heart and the effectual, fervent prayer of a righteous man avails much.

Inner healing is required.

I believe there is a spiritual event and healing that takes place when a fault/wound is confessed with sincerity down into the level of the emotion and the exact wound that needs to be healed. If the confession is made on an "intellectual" level only, it will never be completely healed. Intellectual confession is another word for "mental assent," and is usually an attempt to control the emotions and the healing process so that the confession and the feeling of their exposure and the healing won't go too deep.

You have to realize that on a superficial level, the inner healing that is necessary will not take place. God created confession with the mouth as a vehicle to let go of, expel, and release inner faults. Faults are not just personality deficiencies such as talking too much or over pleasing people. Again, faults are fault lines, breaches, wounds, openings, and piercing.

You would think that when people desire to be healed they would totally open up, but unfortunately they struggle with it. Opening up, for a wounded person:

$$\text{exposure} = \text{unprotected}$$
$$\text{unprotected} = \text{vulnerable}$$
$$\text{vulnerable} = \text{unsafe}$$

The defense walls that have been put in place must be let down or allowed to be entered. During this yielding of your vulnerable inner self, the breaching of the walls (even if willingly) will create discomfort in your emotions, which will make you feel unsafe.

During this process, do not believe that your emotions and discomforts are telling you the truth. These fear-based discomforts are telling you that you are in danger if you open up.

This is exactly why people have to be sedated or put under anesthesia when an invasive medical procedure is being conducted. People feel unsafe and feel that they are being breached and become too afraid. Many people experience anxiety and panic under these conditions.

So during the healing process, you must open up, yield, disregard discomforts, and allow your confession, along with sincerity from the heart level, to go down deep into the labeled hurt or wound and say that you let it go. You should even say with your mouth that you denounce the hurt and its effects on you, and in doing so you are separating yourself from the bond you have made with it and it with you.

You probably do not realize it, but there is a trauma bond created in all unresolved wounds, and it must no longer be validated and supported. You must no longer see yourself as that wounded person and no longer identify with it. Stop saying it is "my" hurt, rejection, fear, etc. and begin to separate your identity from it. Create separation from the wound and the way you see yourself.

Remember the way you see yourself is also called self-image. The wounded person must no longer be your identity and self-image, which was your perceived self-view and perceived view from others. Other people usually do not see you as a wounded person and many don't even care, so if you see yourself that way, then you will wonder what they are thinking about you and you become pre-occupied with it. Let it go and denounce it and no longer bond with it.

The wounded person must no longer be your identity and self-image.

Begin to replace the old self-image with your inherent God-given gifts and personality strengths. When you do this, those gifts will fulfill you and create positive experiences that will begin to influence and form a new self-picture based on you seeing yourself operating in your gifts. This is what God intended for you to experience.

Identify, develop, and use your gifts, not only to help others, but for the healthy, positive image of the real you. Remember, when you let go of the past hurt and wound and everything it meant to you, let it go deep. In most cases it is necessary to cry it out. Most people, especially men, are afraid, reluctant, and certainly uncomfortable to cry it out. In many cases the crying it out feels similar to the exposure felt during the negative experience.

As you are crying it out, the crying and release that comes with it usually comes in waves. This means that you will experience a deep cry from your stomach, chest, and throat area, and then it will subside briefly, then another wave will come up. Allow this to happen until it finishes. Then you will feel free. Afterwards you may also feel a little dizzy, light-headed, tingly, and fatigued. Do not let this concern you. What has happened is that your entire nervous system has just responded and released this "negative charge" in you. It feels much like it would if you just dropped two 50-pound sacks of corn from your shoulders. You are very fatigued and breathing hard from the load you were carrying. However, you also feel the relief from the burden.

As time goes on, you will continue to feel better. Hope and joy will increase, and even the colors in the flowers and trees will look brighter. You will be surprised at your overall outlook improvement. You have been healed. After this, you can begin the process of replacing old patterns with new ones and proceed up the pathway of wholeness.

Personal Faults

I Peter 1:7 says that if we confess our faults one to another we will be healed and restored. Many people are afraid of their faults and are afraid to acknowledge and confess them. Confessing them exposes them and releases them so that the secrecy and power they have over you can be removed. I often say, "Secrecy is the greatest enabler of any destructive behavior."

Faults are not just personality weaknesses. Faults are like fault lines, voids, wounds, and breaches in the self-worth, self-image, emotions, and even the body, that have been created by past hurts, traumas, and personal disappointments in life. Again, faults are not limited to perceived negatives in the personality. They are mostly deep wounds that create wound behaviors that are usually manifested through the personality.

These faults can be triggered because they are unhealed, unstable, not solid, not resolved, and not filled in with some kind of permanent filler (not superficial filler such as "it's in the past"). They create hypersensitivity when the mind is on a topic that is associated in some way with that wound. The person does not have to be aware of the past wound because the hypersensitivity that is associated with the past wound will cause subconscious themes to be triggered by a present tense topic. Whatever the trigger, it will play an internal recording.

You can trigger topics and themes. The themes are birthed and developed from a wound or series of wounds over a period of time, while topics are the people, places, things, or subject matters that, in the present, set off or activate the themes.

Themes usually operate on the subconscious level. For example, a person can be falsely accused and it triggers a feeling of injustice or a feeling of being abused because of the injustice and abuse felt from a past trauma or hurt. The present tense topic triggered the past tense hurt.

These themes are eventually programmed from the conscious mind into the subconscious or even the unconscious mind because they have been practiced over a prolonged time period. Then these themes connect and make association with conscious level triggers that activate them.

WOUNDS AND WOUND BEHAVIORS

A wound behavior is a behavior that you develop and learn during the time that you are wounded. If your negative, traumatic, or hurtful experiences and memories are repressed and the feelings and emotions are suppressed (pushed down inside or minimized), then past wounds and hurts will stay inside of you, masked under a behavior that does not seem to be related.

As we have said, this suppressing makes it difficult for people to connect the dots between the present negative behavior and the past wound. This is further complicated when people harboring the old wound (intentionally or not) are in denial and scared to deal with it because of fear, pride, anger or any other reason.

Unresolved issues in childhood ... carry over into adulthood.

If you avoid resolving the past and remain wounded, the wound does not just disappear over time. It continues through adulthood to negatively influence your behavior, decisions, relationships, attractions, and closeness, in addition to creating a variety of fears.

The unresolved past also creates anxiety that can graduate into panic attacks and disorders. A wound behavior can be any symptomatic behavior that is connected to or birthed from a past wound. Some examples include: anxiety disorders, panic disorders, stress disorders, uncontrolled anger, addictions, self-medicating, self-mutilating, violence, eating disorders, bipolar disorders, phobias, post traumatic stress disorder, obsessions and compulsions (OCD, anxiety, or personality characteristics or disorders) and more.

Furthermore, unresolved past wounds and hurts create fears that the bad experience will happen again. These fears motivate people to construct walls and defenses that become fear-based control mechanisms (see chapter on fear based control mechanisms).

A wound is a painful experience that can be self-inflicted or inflicted by some outside source (person, place, or thing). The pain can be experienced on different levels depending on how it affects the individual and on the depth and duration of the painful experience. Even if five different people experienced the exact same wounding, they would feel it and process it differently.

It is necessary to note that all behaviors that are classified as a "disorder" of some kind do not originate with a wound. Some disorders are brain-chemistry driven. However, a wound can magnify or make chemistry imbalance much worse and much more complicated. For example, a female can have some moderate to severe moods because of neurotransmitter or hormonal imbalances that would not be classified as a disorder. But a wound of some magnitude and the emotional instability created by wounds will drive the intensity and frequency of the imbalance upward to where it could and often does become a disorder. Therefore, wound behavior can include all of the above examples.

TREATMENT

Disorders and non-disorder wound behaviors can be treated with numerous forms of treatments, depending on the thought, emotional, and behavioral instability and/or destructiveness. The particular treatments I personally use in my practice are often treatments that include psychotherapy (resolving the past), cognitive therapy (correct retrain thinking patterns), and behavioral therapy (remove and replace old patterns).

I also include therapy that is spiritual in nature. I do this because I have found, over the last 20 years of private practice and on-site therapy, that a person cannot be completely treated, healed, and restored to a sound mental and emotional state unless you address the spirit of a man or woman. I believe that we, as human beings, are made up of spirit, soul (mind and emotions), and body. Consequently, in order to heal your entire being, you must address your spirit as well. Many counselors do not treat the spirit, thus reducing their ability to go to the depths required to heal some wounds and complications.

In fact, most therapists know there are some behaviors that are so unnatural that they don't know how to address the behavior and the entities they are observing in some of their patients. I believe that in these cases you can only deal with them on a spiritual level because some problems are both spiritual and natural. Another word for spiritual is "supernatural," which is why I used the word "unnatural" to describe it. Because it is not natural, it cannot be effectively addressed by natural therapy and medical remedies.

> To be free, you must open up.

I have treated many patients who not only have a great prognosis, but who also remained healed over years of time, by starting my therapy with confessions to both God and man. When I say confessions, I mean confessions of everything they have ever done in their past that constitutes a wound, a sin, a violation, a hurt, or a trauma.

This confession must include how it negatively affected them (from their perspective). It also includes any other person who was involved or associated with the wound and the details of the event. I have found that when people are willing to go to these radical lengths to be free and healed, they will be. When you want healing on a core deep level, down to the depth of the deepest wound, you must open up to those levels. Otherwise some of the wound and its damage will remain intact inside of you. In a way, you have protected it because of fear or shame. These are the typical reasons why people resist and avoid this deep cleansing and healing.

TRINITY PROGRAM

In addition to the confessions in one-on-one therapy sessions, it may also be necessary to have joint sessions with family or friends to address certain issues. Additionally, I always recommend that my patients and clients attend my Trinity Program, an intense 2½-day training program where our purpose is three fold; resolve your past, restore your health, and retrain your thinking.

The Trinity Program came out of my 20 years of counseling experience from which I realized a need for my clients to go to a deeper place of cleansing, healing, and training than a traditional therapy group or lecture session could provide. The Trinity Program is always held in an upper scale environment that is conducive to relaxation and recovery and includes all meals, elegant meeting rooms, constant beverages, workbooks, Trinity staff and facilitators, special music, and a special fireside attendee's social.

The program is divided into three parts:

Step #1: Resolving your past

Resolving your past involves completing inventories followed by a confession to the small group of all hurts and wounds in your life. This type of confession opens you up to a depth that will bring relief from the fear and shame of the past so you can be healed and restored to a spiritual tone of mind and heart.

Prayer is included during the confession to help you include God in your healing to empower you beyond your mortal human ability for healing and restoration. You will actually experience a genuine natural and spiritual healing as a result of your heart-felt confessions.

During your confessions you will also be led by our facilitators to forgive and receive forgiveness for yourself and others who have hurt or wounded you. Forgiveness does not condone the wounding actions of others, but it does release you from the emotional prison it confines you to.

When you confess to God you experience forgiveness and cleansing (I John 1:9 AMP). When you confess to another human, you experience healing and restoration (James 5:16 AMP). This type of confession works well regardless of your denomination or church affiliation or with no church background or affiliation. All you need is an open and willing heart for life. God is all about life.

Step #2: Restoring your health

Restoring your health includes a restoring and redefining of your self-worth and self-image.

Step #3: Retraining your thinking

Retraining your thinking involves removing old thinking and behavior patterns and replacing them with new ones. During this part of the program you will receive training on a spiritual, psychological, behavioral, and experiential level.

When you have a new positive experience, it provides a new revelation and understanding of how to separate yourself from the old unhealthy you and into the real you. The real you consists of your God-given gifts, talents, and strengths which reside inside of you on a core spiritual DNA level.

When you tap into this real you, it produces success and personal fulfillment in life.

Chapter 6

A Real Story of Resolving the Past

The story you are about to read is from a female patient of mine named "Terri." I chose her story because it will inspire you with hope and faith for your own healing or the healing of a friend or loved one.

Terri went through horrific wounds in her life but came back from the jaws of death on every level to experience healing and restoration that she really never thought possible.

Terri's story

This is a summary of Terri's personal story, written by Terri herself:

> It was late in the summer of 2005 when Dr. Jones and I first spoke. Living in Ohio, isolated from family and friends, I had no desire or inner strength to make the effort to live any longer. The most recent blow was the straw that broke the camel's back for me. I'd been raped by a man to whom I was engaged to be married, another "Christian" male who served as the final proof for me that "men cannot be trusted."
>
> Having failed at attempts to end my life in the past, I had determined that as long as I was still breathing I needed to make myself as unattractive as possible, especially to men. I became obsessed with self-mutilating using lighted cigarettes and sharp objects. I abandoned all grooming and personal hygiene practices.

Death-wishing being deeply ingrained, I regularly and liberally consumed a toxic cocktail of alcohol and prescription medications in a deliberate effort to poison my liver.

By the time I had my first phone appointment with Dr. Jones, my arms and legs were riddled with cigarette burns and lacerations. A couple of months earlier, my mom had made a trip from Virginia to scoop me up and take me to Cleveland Clinic where I stayed in detox for about a month. I'd been completely intoxicated for over a year, drinking as many as 18 12-oz bottles of beer daily. While the hospital environment and medical staff helped me to stop abusing my body with alcohol, it provided no lasting hope that life for me would get any better or that the fear and emotional pain I'd carried deep inside since I was a young child would ever really go away. I still had no vision, no hope, and no desire to live. In order to help you understand why, allow me to tell you a little about myself.

I was an unplanned, unwanted pregnancy. My young mother already had one son and one daughter and had absolutely no desire for any more children. I remember as a child often hearing my mom tell me the story of how she fell in love the moment she laid eyes on this beautiful baby girl. Though her intent was to express how precious I was to her, the message I heard was that "appearances matter most" and mine would always play a pivotal role in serving to validate (or invalidate) my very existence. In my childish understanding, I was rejected until my physical features were seen and approved. This false belief would become deeply entrenched as future experiences would only serve to "prove" they were correct.

When I was about eight or nine years of age, my dad began grooming me for his own personal sexual gratification. Though he may not have been the first man to exploit me in a sexual nature (my earliest memory is of an adult male who lived across the street when I was about five years of age who taught my friend and me a "more fun way" to play "hide-and-go-seek"), my dad's abuse was understandably the most impacting. Other than these times, the attention I received from him was rare, except for purposes of correction or discipline.

This induced a confusing mixture of excitement and guilt associated with the molestations. I craved my dad's acceptance, approval, and affection and this was the closest I could come to getting it. At the same time, his unnatural behavior and unpredictable anger terrified me to the core. His acts of sexual abuse toward me ended when I was about 14 years of age. That night, I found my voice as I heard myself ask him to please stop. He retreated to his room in disgrace and tears while I ran to my older sister in guilt and terror. My mother had separated from my dad temporarily and was staying with a friend, so my sister was the only recourse I had at that moment for comfort and help.

While she tried to decipher my words between sobs, my dad was in his room packing a bag to leave. That was one of my biggest fears, that if I ever spoke up it would tear this already fractured family apart once and for all. I hated what my dad had done to me, but I loved him. I didn't want that to happen.

When my sister finally got the gist of what I was trying to tell her, she hugged me and told me she understood ... he'd done the same thing to her. Suddenly, it occurred to me that he may have left. I ran into his room just in time to catch him before he slipped out the side door of his home office. With his suitcase in one hand and the other on the door knob, I grabbed him and begged him not to go. He wept shamefully, not understanding how I could possibly want him to stay.

Meanwhile, my sister called the church and some of the leaders came to our home. While they spent most of their time talking with my dad, one of them slipped over to me and said, "You know you need to forgive your father, don't you?"

I responded emphatically, "Yes! Of course I do!"

Having been raised in the church, this was one thing I understood well, that in order to be forgiven one must be willing to forgive. Over the course of the next several months though, I noticed a growing rage inside of me that wouldn't go away no matter what I did. I thought it meant I hadn't forgiven him. Too ashamed and embarrassed to tell anyone, I kept a tight rein on it while I privately and repeatedly begged God to help me and take the anger away. At the same time, I was elated over the fact that my dad and I were building a relationship together. He had been receiving counseling ministry through the church, my mom had returned to me, and it was beginning to feel like I had a real family.

However, this newfound sense of excitement and hope came to an abrupt halt less than a year later. Following a late dinner one evening, my dad asked if I'd like to join him for a trip to his office to pick up some things. On the way back home, he drove around aimlessly under the guise of just wanting to spend time with me. I could tell something wasn't right. He took me to a park where there in the darkness he attempted to seduce me. Once again, I was terrified of my own father. I managed to maintain a composed facade as I sat there reminding him of all the right reasons to do the right thing, throwing in a few scriptures for the benefit of conviction. Nothing happened. Not physically anyway. But emotionally I became more confused and afraid than ever.

The following three years, I was a conflicted soul leading a very contradictory lifestyle. I still believed in Jesus as my Savior and wanted with all my heart to serve the Lord, but the internal rage was quickly evolving into a fiery inferno and becoming more and more difficult to conceal or control. There was no middle ground for me. Sometimes I was totally sold out for Christ and living in an extremely legalistic manner in ways like not allowing myself to wear makeup, pulling my hair back into a tight bun, and poring over the scriptures for hours at a time on a daily basis.

But when I couldn't be perfect, I'd go to the opposite extreme. At 16, I began sleeping around and even experimented with a lesbian relationship. By the age of 19, I found myself pregnant. This was a huge wake-up call and I once again committed my life to God. After doing the math, I married the man I believed was most likely the father. The baby girl I carried inside me for nine months died six days after birth from a rare heart condition.

I was sure God was punishing me and equally sure I deserved it. Two years later, a son was born into a very tumultuous relationship. I'd already been diagnosed with bipolar disorder and by then I was no longer able to hide the fury that consumed me. What my heart wanted for my son was a healthy, normal Christian family, but even with counseling, therapy, and professional help, I was incapable of doing anything remotely close to making that a reality. Instead, we were dysfunctional and fragmented, just like the family into which I'd been born.

After 12 years of hell on earth, I separated from my husband and we divorced five years later. During the separation, I had to have a hysterectomy. Following this operation, between the manic-depressive episodes, imbalanced hormones, and a desperate need for emotional healing, I literally went off the deep end. It seemed as though I spent almost as much time in hospital psyche wards as out of them.

Once more, I began living the life of a person who could call herself anything but a Christian. After the divorce was final, I tried again to lead a Christ-centered life. Not much time passed before I fell in love with a man I had met on a Christian website. He lived in a different state and had a young son. We decided to get married and agreed that, between the two of us, it was more practical for me to move where he lived as he shared custody of his son with his ex-wife. By that time, my son wanted little or nothing to do with me and I'd given up on even trying to be his mother anymore. He was 15 when I moved to Ohio.

Dr. Jones was just another man as far as I was concerned. Regardless of his credentials or the success he'd had with other clients, who may have been as bad as or worse off than me, I didn't trust him. After all, I'd had plenty of counseling throughout my life by both professionals and ministers, some of whom had made sexual advances themselves while they were supposed to be helping me to heal and get past the abuse I'd endured as a child. This, naturally, further augmented my deep-seated suspicions toward any person of the male gender.

The only reason I was willing to talk to Dr. Jones at all was because my mother had very lovingly persuaded me to do so "just one time." That one time became a one-at-a-time phone appointment, which eventually led to my coming to Texas to see him in person for an intense three weeks of appointments, about four days per week, each lasting anywhere from two to six hours.

It was then that I first became exposed to some of the life-changing concepts that Dr. Jones teaches and uses in his Trinity Program. Less than three months later, in March of 2006, I moved back to San Antonio, Texas (my place of birth and where I'd spent most of my life) so that I could continue seeing him on a regular basis. That was when I began to become more aware of the principles behind his Resolve/Restore/Retrain course of therapy.

We began the process of step one (resolve the past) by isolating and identifying each and every memory associated with past hurts, wounds, traumas, and disappointments, and following scriptural principles and guidelines for addressing each one individually.

Once I had effectively forgiven my offenders and confessed and repented of my own sinful responses to each of them, I was able to move forward in the direction of healing through step two (restore to health). During this part of the process, I learned the difference between self-worth (which is determined by God and fixed in eternity) and self-image (my personal perception of my worth or value). I began to replace false beliefs about who I am with the truth of what God's Word says about me.

From there, I transitioned into the final stage of my journey to wholeness through step three (retrain the mind) by identifying and intentionally removing negative thought and behavior patterns and replacing them with new productive thought processes and conduct.

It wasn't all as neat and tidy as that last paragraph may seem to indicate. I was a mess. Furthermore, I am by no means saying that I've "arrived." I'm a firm believer that on this side of Heaven we must continually strive to forgive and let go, to learn and grow. The tools I was given through Dr. Jones are as valuable in my life today as the first day they were made available to me nearly six years ago and the Holy Spirit patiently teaches me how to implement them effectively on a daily basis.

The main difference is that there finally exists in my life a firm foundation of truth and I have confidence and hope that whatever God desires to build on it will remain stable. I have a feeling Jesus would agree that it was worth every drop of blood, sweat and tears to get me to this place.

Q & A with Terri

Question: How did you process out of this?

Terri: At the risk of sounding cliché, it truly was "one day at a time." The Lord knows how much each of us can handle at any given moment and for me there was an immense amount of grace, especially in the initial stages. When we make the decision to trust Him and we stand in that decision, only good can come of it.

I can't say I understood from the beginning the method Dr. Jones had the wisdom to exercise. I was so desperate though, that as long as what he was giving me as instruction to do seemed morally and spiritually sound and I was able to do it, I knew it was necessary to trust the Lord and follow His guidance through this man.

My senses were pretty finely tuned to the immoral nature of fallen creation. I believe that, in light of what I desired to accomplish and the critical state I was in, God would have protected me had Dr. Jones been just another in a long line of men with selfish or impure motives. Thankfully, he is a man of integrity and of good moral fiber. He clearly has a heart after God.

Question: What were the stages of coming out of it?

Terri: I had a lot of addictions and negative behaviors to overcome. At first, we dealt with some of the worst of these, including the suicidal thoughts and self-mutilation. Since this part of the process took place while I still lived in Ohio, he had me take pictures of my arms which was where I focused most of my attention when burning or cutting myself, then send them to him via my camera-phone.

We spoke almost every day and I knew each time I'd be giving an account of my activities with regards to caring for these self-inflicted wounds. (I was instructed to wash and disinfect them regularly, followed by an application of Vitamin-E oil used also as an anointing oil, while I prayed over myself.) I came to learn that he'd also be asking regularly whether or not I had any fresh wounds. Knowing I'd be telling him one way or the other made it less difficult to abstain from that temptation.

Since I had become so isolated, Dr. Jones also spent time retraining me to live in a more functionally-normal manner, which included some of the most basic daily activities such as bathing/showering, brushing my teeth, and wearing clean clothes. These activities may be second nature to someone who has never abandoned their practice but for me it meant choosing to give caring attention to this body I had so long neglected and tried to destroy. It was an exercise completely unsupported by my emotions at the time.

In the beginning, I wept bitterly through the steps of personal hygiene, but I did it anyway. (Ever tried brushing your teeth while crying?) Each time I followed through, there was a sense of accomplishment and relief and the next time was less difficult.

When I was forced to leave my apartment, I felt safest under the cloak of darkness. Prior to Dr. Jones's involvement in my recovery, my practice had been to go shopping or to the liquor store in the middle of the night when I was least likely to run into anyone who knew me. This was an especially big deal for me. The very thought of possibly being seen or recognized would send my thoughts into a dangerous downward spiral. He was sensitive to this and helped me to take baby steps in the direction of deliverance from this tormenting fear.

One such step was my agreement to go to the small library down the street to use the computer so I could email updates to him on the days we didn't speak by phone. I also began keeping praise and worship music playing in my apartment non-stop day and night which served as spiritual encouragement, reinforcement, and warfare on my behalf.

Much like gradually adding weight to one's workout routine for the purpose of building strength and endurance, Dr. Jones broadened his attention to more issues at a time as he discerned I was ready to deal with them. Meanwhile, I was developing a stronger walk with the Lord and learning again to trust my ability to hear His Voice.

There were setbacks. I've always been rather stubborn and I'd frequently succumb to the fears, giving Dr. Jones a real run for his money. He remained patient and faithful.

Question: What were your thoughts?

Terri: At first they were very much the same as what they had always been. It was a moment-by-moment struggle to retrain my thinking. My core beliefs were pretty much set in stone and they weren't going to be excavated and replaced without patient persistence and sheer determination.

Here again is where the importance of faith and trust in God is crucial. When God says one thing but everything within us is screaming the opposite, it's time to make a choice. Who will we believe? I knew that what I'd believed and done up to that point had failed me utterly and completely, and that if things were going to change I would have to allow that change to transpire from the inside out. That required literally trading my thoughts about everything and everyone, including myself, for my Creator's thoughts.

For example, there were times I thought I'd die (literally) before I would see evidence that a transformation was taking place. I felt it intensely! My thoughts were telling me to run, to get away from the danger! But Dr. Jones had prepared me for this in advance and I was duly equipped. When the time came, it was simply a matter of following through with what I'd agreed to do in just such a scenario. Gradually, the old was being replaced with the new and doing these things came more and more naturally.

Question: How did it feel?

Terri: I'm somewhat apprehensive to answering this question. On the one hand, I don't want the facts to deter anyone who desires to courageously take this promising path toward healing and restoration. Yet my answer should be honest and forthright. I started to say that it isn't for the faint of heart but the truth is, that's exactly who it's for! Our Heavenly Father is so ready and able to be the strength that we need in order to survive and thrive through an otherwise impossible situation!

The times I am made most aware of His tremendous affections for me are when I am weakest and least equipped in any given situation. His love is magnified when our humanness requires His intervention. So regardless of how it feels, it's more than doable and so very, very worth the effort.

In short, it felt at times like I wouldn't make it until the end. Often I just wanted to give up. In many instances I nearly did. Digging deep down inside ourselves, removing barricades to dark places we spend our lives trying to forget are there, allowing God access to the most sensitive areas ... these are arduous exercises.

Going through more pain to obtain healing when pain is what we want so desperately to escape seems contradictory and is certainly not an appealing thought, I know. I felt and expressed every negative emotion I'd ever experienced. That particular action put me face to face with the reality of just how ugly I am apart from Him. Yet in the midst of all of the emotional wreckage, the Lord faithfully appeared on the scene at every single appointment! I had only to be open to the Spirit of God as He poured His healing oil over freshly exposed virulent wounds, some of which had been there since childhood.

When we began transitioning into the second and third stages of my healing journey, I went from being eager for an appointment to end to being disappointed it was over so quickly. For the first time in my life, I was discovering the me I was created to be, learning about my giftings and how they can best be used to glorify God, and gaining fresh insights into the practical application of scriptural principles in my everyday life. There was a dramatic 180 degree shift in my outlook. My entire perspective had changed from what it had been only a few months earlier.

I'm going to borrow an over-used adage here because it so appropriately sums up this whole experience for me: It was as though I'd been given a new lease on life.

Question: What were some of your spiritual revelations?

Terri: I referred primarily to the sexual abuse in my past when telling my story because it is what left the most obvious collateral damage. But there were numerous other issues (especially from during my primary years of emotional development) that needed to be addressed as well. Both my father and mother had each also suffered a variety of abuses and neglect as children. They entered marriage and parenthood with no healing and without any real direction as to how to break this evil cycle. Sadly, the church was not equipped to handle such problems in a truly effective manner.

No matter how noble or pure our intentions may be, we will continue to inflict pain on others as long as we harbor unhealed wounds within ourselves. Over the course of my treatment I became increasingly aware of this fact. Realizing this certainly makes it easier to swallow the forgiveness pill. It also serves as a consistent reminder of the importance of cleaning up any fresh injuries as soon as possible not only for my own sake but for the sake of not perpetuating the offense, especially onto innocent bystanders.

But is forgiveness simply a matter of accepting that it is a requirement for followers of Christ and thereby choosing to comply? This is a delicate subject with many different scriptural angles from which it must be evaluated. Admittedly, I still wrestle to fully comprehend what God's Word has to say concerning this matter but I said something when telling part of my story and would like to revisit there in hopes of sharing some of the light I believe God has shed on this matter for me thus far.

I told about the time the church leaders visited in the middle of the same night that I finally "found my voice." They were mostly trying to minister to my dad while I sat across the room pretty much in shock over all that had transpired. When one of them came and reminded me of my need to forgive my father, I adamantly stated my agreement. That was the response of a very confused young teenage girl who just wanted to do the right thing. I did believe I needed to forgive him and at that point believed that I had. Oh, that it were so simple!

Perhaps there are times in which God dispenses a special kind of grace that enables one to forgive life-altering offenses so quickly and easily, but that was not the case for me in this situation. After many years of torment and self-condemning thoughts and actions over the fact that my feelings did not match up with my profession of forgiveness, it occurred to me that my belief system may be faulty.

Even then, it was many more years before I would actually begin to explore that possibility. The idea that the foundational beliefs upon which my entire life rested could contain critical flaws meant reexamining what I believed and why I believed it and allowing God, through His Word, to expose areas of deception. During my execution of this endeavor, I have indeed discovered errors (or apparently huge gaps in some arenas) in my basic theological understanding of some very key principles in God's Word, forgiveness being one of them.

As I indicated earlier, I don't claim to have all the answers. On the contrary, I'm still very much in search mode. However, there are some insights I've come to discover along the way that have brought with them a measure of peace; the kind of peace to which I believe Paul was referring in Philippians 4:7 where it says: "And the peace of God, which transcends all understanding, will guard your hearts and your minds in Christ Jesus."

> Concerning the matter of forgiveness, I'm learning that it can sometimes be an involved process that doesn't necessarily all happen at the moment we choose to forgive. Of course, that moment of choice is crucial and is the starting place which serves as our point of reference when the enemy comes with an accusing finger pointed at the unfinished parts of our transformation. When that happens, and it most surely will happen, we are once more given the opportunity to exercise our faith over our feelings. Acceptance that this is often a progressive development that takes place over time can help to dispel false feelings of guilt (not to be mistaken for true Holy

Spirit conviction) that may be associated with unresolved emotions, but it should by no means become an excuse to act out unforgiving behaviors toward the offending party. Exercising my will by making the choice to obediently forgive regardless of my emotional status is, in essence, a seed planted. As I consistently care for and diligently water that seed (meditation on and agreement with God's Word is fundamentally vital here), the fruit of that obedience will manifest eventually. The most challenging part of this particular revelation has been adopting it and allowing it to replace certain old beliefs and patterns of behavior regarding forgiveness.

Question: What was the journey? Did you develop new logic or new thoughts?

Terri: The journey continues. As described previously, the start was a rough one. The repercussions that developed from my childhood traumas included a warped perspective of life, distrust (especially toward men and God), and chemical imbalances leading to psychological illnesses such as bipolar and obsessive-compulsive disorders, which further resulted in years of dependence on antidepressant, anti-anxiety, and various other mood stabilizing prescription drugs.

In addition, some of the destructive habit patterns that emerged included isolating, self-mutilating, "death-wishing," suicide attempts, and addictive behaviors such as cigarette smoking and excessive consumption of alcohol. It goes without saying that Dr. Jones had his work cut out for him. He wisely chose his battles. Obviously, it was important to address all of the unhealthy thoughts and behaviors, but to have attempted to do so all at once would have sent me running. The saying, "If you want to take a bone from a dog, offer him a piece of meat," comes to mind.

This would be a good place to mention the consistent sensitivity Dr. Jones has to the Spirit of God. His level of spiritual discernment at times is uncanny. I say this not to exalt the man, but rather the One to Whom he yields. Often, I witnessed as he would briefly pause, close his eyes and tilt his head slightly to one side and upward as though stretching to completely grasp a fresh revelation. While these kinds of gestures and mannerisms may easily be performed of one's own volition, such voided displays would fail to accompany the massive results like those that have reverberated in my life far beyond the close of our sessions. Time after time, I was the blessed recipient of the move of the Spirit through an anointed man of God. This is what earned him my ultimate trust and, more importantly, renewed my trust in God.

Once we had established the initial points of reference for forgiveness and repentance (this practice continued as a kind of clean-up at the close of most appointments), we delved further into the issues that had stunted my growth and handicapped my level of functioning, majoring on any viewpoints that were diametrically opposed to Scriptural truth. After the more obvious hindrances were tackled, we honed in on the less conspicuous deceptions that had been misshaping my perceptions.

Eventually, addictions such as smoking were resolved. Surprisingly, Dr. Jones himself never once addressed that issue. Perhaps he understood that when I was ready, the Lord would move on me concerning the need to trust Him with any remaining anxieties that kept me chained to this potentially fatal habit. That is exactly how it happened too. But even before that, another longtime prayer of mine was answered.

I had long desired to be freed from reliance on prescription drugs. Bipolar disorder is generally regarded to be a condition one is not likely to get over. Once diagnosed, you're branded for life. Furthermore, withdrawal from the medications is no small matter. To be able to discontinue their use would be truly liberating but I knew I was asking for a minor miracle. As my therapy progressed and the fruit was becoming more apparent, my faith that this could actually happen grew stronger.

Eventually, after much prayer, I began a gradual step-down process. Over the period of the next 13 months my miracle was unfolding, until one day, I was completely unshackled! It's been nearly two years now since I've taken any psychotropic drugs.

The best part is that I've never felt more "normal" than I do now. I would be remiss in not telling you that doing this was neither suggested by Dr. Jones nor was he involved in the process. The therapy I received through him merely became the catalyst for my growing faith. It is also not something that should be pursued without medical supervision.

Several factors played into my eventual healing on my journey to wholeness, but none more important than my willingness to comply. Even with all the correct ingredients and proper tools, a meal does not prepare itself. That's not to say I was always happily compliant. Operating from a distrustful outlook, gripping fear, and a general sense of despair for so many years, those negative characteristics were destined to interfere with an otherwise ideally smooth progression. Dr. Jones practiced remarkable discernment and godly wisdom (and did I mention patience?) in response to each of my self-sabotaging attempts to impede success.

I'm no mason, but I believe the task of tearing down old crumbling fortresses and rebuilding them brick by brick would be a good analogy for the work Dr. Jones did with me. At first, laying one or two blocks at a time was quite the undertaking, but as we progressed there were occasions when entire sections were forged in a single session.

Now it is my turn for a cliché ... you wouldn't recognize Terri today if you saw her! God's handiwork is amazing!

CHAPTER 7

PRACTICAL NEXT STEPS TO BEING FREE OF YOUR PAST

The testimony of Terri is very powerful, moving, and inspiring. Terri was seemingly destined to die early in life and if not, she would be alive physically but in constant misery, torment, and darkness. But instead, she has profoundly changed from death to life.

I often tell my clients to choose life and not death in every aspect of their life. Always ask yourself the question, "Will this decision produce life or death in me?"

For most of Terri's past existence, experiencing life was something that was nowhere remotely in the radar of her biggest imaginations or desperate cries. But both a spiritual and a natural transformation has taken place in her on all levels: spiritually, emotionally, mentally, and physically. You can experience this kind of deep change in you, even if your problems are not as severe or even if they are worse than Terri's.

SPIRITUAL TRANSFORMATION

Spiritual transformation takes place in your spirit, which is the core real you. God is a spirit. When His Spirit comes in contact with yours at your request, you will experience a true transformation. This experience is different than a dry and religious church service that bores you and never really dips down inside of you and produces any life, faith, or empowerment.

As a therapist who hears people's true, honest, and most radical thoughts, most people long for and wish there was a God who could deliver them from their misery and their mediocre existence and cleanse them from their wounds. Well, He does exist and His love, life, and light will do just that for you personally! When you experience the real Him, you will know the difference between man's religion with rules, demands, dictates, and condemnation, and a powerful yet loving God.

If you have doubts about this, I challenge you to ask Him to make Himself real to you in any way He chooses and see what happens. All you have to do is sincerely ask and you will have experiences that are spiritual, but not harmful or unsafe to you. Just because you cannot see God with your physical eyes does not mean He does not exist. He is very aware of who you are.

> **Will this decision produce life or death in me?**

The physical eye can only see visible light, yet visible light only represents approximately 5% of the known light or electromagnet energy that is in existence. Humans utilize and benefit from these light/energy sources constantly. These light/energy wavelengths make up the following light sources: near and far infrared, radio waves, microwaves, ultraviolet, x-ray, gamma rays, and more. You cannot see these sources with your human visible imaging capabilities, but with assistance you can not only see these wavelengths, but can benefit from them. Used within their designed purpose, they are productive. Used outside of their designed purpose, they are destructive. They can help you or hurt you depending on what you do with them and your understanding of them.

God and His angels cannot be seen by human eyes, but this does not mean that He does not exist or that He can't help you. The fact is that He can and will put life in you when you ask Him to come inside of you. It's more than just "helping" you, it's you experiencing Him.

Fear is a lie

When you practice a fear, the fear can turn into a belief that the fear is telling you the truth. The more you practice and validate fear and its messages, the more you will believe that being afraid protects you from the things you fear.

If you are afraid of the unknown, for example, that fear will eventually create an actual belief that you really are unprotected and unsafe if you have too many unknowns. You will believe that being afraid protects you by keeping you on high alert. However, that state of high alert will also keep you from sleeping at night, you will develop phobias, you will obsess over missing some details, and eventually it will control your mind and rob your peace.

When I talk about unknowns, I'm not telling you to not know about your expenses, income, and where your children are. I am talking about what being afraid does to you. It will make you believe that if you are not afraid, then you are missing some detail that will create some danger or risk for you, when those details within themselves are not that important. This kind of obsessing makes you controlling and micromanaging in the way you conduct your affairs and in your relationships.

When these types of fear-based control mechanisms are used, they create a false sense of comfort. The fears tell you that if you increase the "known's" and decrease the amount of unknowns, then you are safe. Unfortunately, you are never able to know everything in advance. Consequently, fear will always make you feel that you are missing some details and that, unless you get the details, you have loose ends. This will create anxiety if you are not in control in some way.

Control-oriented fears will eventually torment you because you can never satisfy the fear long enough to have permanent peace. These controls can include controlled environments, limited friends, limited or no socializing, and no spontaneous decisions to do anything. Again, this controlled environment gives you the feeling that you are safer in some way because there are no unknowns.

An example of a person using control mechanisms to protect from something they are afraid of is seen in a wife who will not allow herself to be exposed at a deep emotional level through any kind of intimacy. She even avoids conversations about herself in order to not be vulnerable. In doing so, she falsely believes that if she keeps her distance (even with someone who loves her and would not hurt her), then her spouse can never get close enough to really know her faults and therefore never find out she is not good enough, which is what she believes about herself. Therefore she will be in less danger to be rejected if no one gets too close. Her fear, she believes, is protecting her.

All of the activity I have just described to you occurs on the subconscious level, but by explaining it I am bringing it up to the conscious level so that the fear can be exposed and dismantled. Dismantling fear messages is essential in being free from the fears and the dictates of the fear. As I stated, fear lies and fear has rules and requirements that confine you and keep you in a "box." You are not protected by the fear. Fear does not protect. If fear legitimately protected us, then every Navy Seal or Army Special Ops team would be taught to fear as soon as they reached boot camp in order to protect and maximize their capabilities and fulfill their purpose. On the contrary, they are equipped with the knowledge of combat, weapons, and efficiency under stress and real danger.

If you use control mechanisms to feel safe, then the controls actually begin to control you. This is because if you do not use control, then you feel unprotected and even unsafe. Consequently, you begin to obey the fear-based controls and the

> **Control-oriented fears will eventually torment you.**

requirements of the control mechanisms. At this point the fear-based controls are controlling you and if you do not "obey" the dictates and confines of the controls, then you feel out of control, not in control, or being controlled. When you feel this way, you are uncomfortable. When you get back within the control boundaries, then the discomfort subsides or is reduced.

This is what I call "the box." If you get outside of the box or confines of control, you feel uncomfortable. So in order to feel comfortable, you must get back into the box. You must obey the box and not violate its boundaries and comfort zones if you don't want to feel discomfort. You are no longer doing the controlling, but rather the fear-based controls are controlling you.

Fear infects the conscience

Just like any behavior, when fears are practiced over a period of time, the mind eventually downloads the fears into the subconscious and unconscious level. When this happens, the fear thoughts (messages), behaviors, and emotions become automatic behavior. When this fear is physically practiced, then the central nervous system programs the fear as normal and encodes or remembers it so that it can express it again and again without conscious, pre-meditated thought or intent at the time of the behavior.

> **Fears actually end up controlling the person who is fearful.**

At this point, the fear integrates into the actual conscience and redefines the conscience. This is possible because fear can create comfort zones that can be perceived as right and wrong. This also happens because fear can redefine the definition and the difference between right and wrong.

For example, if you used to think it was right to socialize on a superficial or acquaintance level, a fear of rejection would tell you that it is wrong to socialize and you would reduce your socializing and openness. The fear tells you that openness means exposure and vulnerability means you are unprotected. Then you obey the fear and eventually think it is wrong to socialize and you begin to isolate more in an attempt to make yourself feel safer on some level.

As I have previously stated, the fear tells people to control more, but the fear actually ends up controlling them because it restricts movement so that there are less unknowns.

The more territory you have to be exposed to, the more potential there is for unknowns, and unknowns create the fear of hidden dangers of some kind. The fear tells or prompts you to reduce your territory, and in doing so, it supposedly reduces your unknowns.

Fear also infects and redefines the conscience by creating guilt or self-accusations that you have done something wrong when you really have not. An example of this is when parents become afraid that their children will be hit by a car in the street and start out not allowing their children to play in any street (even a remote side street, even under close supervision), then not allowing them to play near the street, then not allowing them to play in the front yard, and then not allowing them outside.

At the point when parents feel they are doing wrong if they violate the fear boundaries and rules, fear has successful redefined their conscience or the definitions of right and wrong.

This is why I teach that fear is not a healthy protector. Fear is a tormentor that will control people's lives and decisions and happiness. I am often asked, "What is the healthy way to protect and make decisions?" The four healthy protectors are knowledge, wisdom, understanding, and discretion (more about this in the Retraining the Mind section).

THE PROCESS OF RESOLVING YOUR PAST

This process requires that your past hurts, traumas, wounds, and disappointments be identified, forgiven, healed, and processed correctly in your mind and perceptions. Are you bound and held captive to your past unnecessarily? If so, this will cause you to constantly look back in regret, guilt, shame, fear, or self-condemnation.

Looking back and examining the past is only productive if you confess your mistakes, sins, and bad choices for the purpose of resolving them and learning to never repeat the same patterns again. Your memory was not created to rehash the past in order to self-punish and self-condemn. It was created to be used as a reference point for improvement.

Rehashing the past negative information over and over, but never coming up with a solution or closure, will produce torment but no positive change. That torment will create fear, which is often generated in the present because of past tense negative experiences. That fear typically manifests itself as a fear of the unknown which, as you know, feeds off of past unresolved negative experiences by wondering if they will happen again. The fear of them happening again has power because there is no resolve, and therefore keeps it empowered in you.

You must complete the process of resolving the past and stop tormenting yourself by rehearsing the same past information over and over, but never coming up with a solution. There is always a solution if you want one and closure can be attained.

> **There is always a solution if you want one.**

Scripture says to seek and you shall find, knock and it shall be opened to you. Seeking does require some action. The fear will speak to you and tell you not to open up the past just to ignore it because it is in the past, but the reality is that just because something happened in the past does not mean it stays in the past. The past will speak and influence in the future through fears and wound-behaviors that must be dealt with. Open the closet and clean out the "skeletons." If there are no skeletons in the closet, then they can't speak to you and you won't have to hold the door closed.

Step #1: Acknowledge

By acknowledging the past wounds (recent or distant) and the way it hurt you and what it has done to you, you can label all the elements of it correctly.

This is necessary because when you remove and resolve something, you must accurately identify why and how you arrived at that point of being wounded so that you will not repeat the wound.

Additionally, you have to know what you are confessing, forgiving, and removing. There must be a conscious, real-time awareness of what condition you are in so you can heal it. A physician's diagnoses for the purpose of knowing what to treat and how to treat it. Emotional and mental wounds, hurts and traumas are the same in that regard.

Step #2: Confess

Confess the wound and hurt and how it affected you. Label it correctly. If you were rejected by family, then say what the rejection was and how it damaged you or created problems for you.

Do not rationalize away when you are resolving and confessing how you have been wounded or how you have wounded others. Make your confession with sincerity of heart (deeper than the intellect). You may not be sure that you can forgive and let it go, but just make the confession with sincerity and faith at the time of the confession. Do it this way even if you are uncertain whether or not you can maintain forgiveness.

Step #3: Forgive (God, self, others)

Sometimes people are angry with God as a result of pain from their own wounds. They feel like God abandoned them.

Consequently, they must forgive God in order to release themselves and also to have a relationship with God.

Step #4: Let Go

Letting go involves releasing the debt you have held against a person or against yourself. Many times people can manage to forgive others of horrible things, but can't seem to release the debt they hold against themselves.

Say with your mouth, "I forgive myself and let go of the debt I have held against myself." This kind of release allows you to let go of the past and stop living in the past. It creates a new reference point from which to proceed forward.

Step #5: Denounce & Create Separation

When you verbally denounce the wound and emotions related to it (unforgiveness, hurt, anger, rage, hate, resentment, inferiority, unsafe, victimized, failure, offense, etc.), you create separation between yourself and the wound.

Many times you can identify and bond with the wound and take it into your identity. It helps when you actually say, "I denounce…" and label the wound and emotions it created.

It also helps cancel any spoken or unspoken vows that you spoke around the time of the wound and the pain. Examples of this kind of vow would be words such as, "I'll never love again" or "I'll never let anyone get that close" or "I have been hurt for the last time" or "I'll pay them back" or "I give up."

Step #6: Heal

Healing is a process. Just like a physical wound requires a healing process, so do emotional wounds. If someone cut your arm, it would take time to heal, but it would also require cleansing the wound, stitching it up, keeping it clean, and protecting it from more harm. Over time it would completely heal with no more pain associated with it, unless of course it was cut open again or the wound was opened up again by another trauma.

> **Relax … recovery and restoration takes time.**

Now, if the same person, your brother as an example, kept wounding you, then it would be normal for you to not trust him when he got near you, even if he said he loved you. Furthermore, if someone else opened up your wound again, you would begin to not trust people being close to you in order to protect yourself from more wounds.

The same is true whether the wound was physical, emotional, or mental. This is why one spouse may not trust the other spouse if the wounding has occurred repeatedly. Then even if the aggressor apologizes and the victim forgives, trust is still not capable of being present in the victim because he or she has been wounded and is still recovering.

Recovery takes time and effort. Some men say, "Why don't you just forgive me?"

Then the wife replies, "I do forgive you."

And then the man wonders why she doesn't act the same toward him. The answer is that she is still healing and it takes time, and she is still protecting herself by distancing herself. This response is normal recovery behavior.

Healing requires that you identify the wound, label it, admit it hurt you, denounce it (so you won't bond with it), and then give it the necessary time for you to process out of it. You should also tell God, and others, that you place the cares of it (worries, anxieties, fear, burdens, and concerns) into God's hands and off of your shoulders. This creates a mental picture of you actually going through that exercise.

Some people even choose to create a stage where they physically act out a demonstration of taking a heavy weight off their shoulders and giving it to someone or putting it some place that represents God physically taking it from them.

Healing also requires that you stop practicing any behaviors that assisted in wounding you and replace those behaviors with new productive ones. This empowers you to take charge of your healing rather than feeling helpless and victimized.

Recovery and restoration take time. Often there is grieving involved in healing and recovery. Grieving is a process that requires working through the past regrets, memories, pain, loneliness, fears, past wounds, and separation.

Remember, during these times, I encourage you to get closer to God and ask and allow Him to help you heal. You are not powerful enough to heal alone. You must have other people and have God to help you where you cannot help yourself. It is okay to not be strong enough alone. There is no shame in allowing people to help you. Humble yourself, let go of the pride or embarrassment, and ask for help. You will find more mercy than you may think.

A) Go to the place of the emotional pain within the wound and release those emotions. This usually results in some form of tears. Crying is not a sign of weakness. God created tears, in this case, as a form of cleansing. Do not suppress the tears by swallowing or holding your breath. Allow yourself to cry as deeply as you can and keep it flowing until it is empty. Give yourself plenty of time to be broken and cry it out. This type of crying breaks the protective wall surrounding the wound and the pain. Allow yourself to be broken so that you can be built back up and restored to health and wholeness. It will feel good to feel good!

Remember, the purpose for this type of crying is not to agonize over the wound and the pain, but to release it. Let it come out of you. Don't keep it inside. It must come out, so tap down into the hurt and emotional place of the wound and let it drain out of you. The emotional place in the wound usually feels powerful because it has energy locked into it as well as memories of the pain related to it.

Neurotransmitters have energy in them, but when a wound is unresolved, it keeps that negative energy locked up inside of the wound. When you go into the emotional place of the wound and allow yourself to remember it, the emotion will begin to come up from down inside of your stomach and up through your throat. When this happens, you must allow yourself to relax as much as possible, open your mouth, breathe, and cry it out. This will be a form of release and relief for you.

Many people swallow the emotions back down and, consequently, keep it inside of them. Many are concerned about how it will feel or sound as they cry out the old wound. At this point, let it happen and realize that the sound is a natural part of the release. In fact you can often tell what emotional hurt and wound is being released by the sound of it. Grief, hurt, hate, sorrow, and others usually have their own distinct sound when being released. Do not be afraid of it. Releasing the pain will not hurt you. However, keeping it inside of you will hurt you and will also manifest as outward behavior.

Again, allow the emotion of it to "come up" so the negative energy can be released. When you release the emotion of the wound, you will typically feel temporary pain or discomfort, but the pain and discomfort will subside as you release it.

B) Trace it back in your memory until you can find it and see the experience in your mind's eye. It helps to go into your memory and identify the wound's "origination point," which is the first time it happened to you. You may be afraid that that will relive it, but you will not relive it. You will, instead, release it.

During this time you will probably feel uncomfortable, but don't be afraid of it. It is normal and the discomfort will subside after you go through this process. It is like a type of surgery where you go in and remove something that is bad for you. Oftentimes clients tell me that surgery is easier because you get to have anesthesia. You will get through it and the pain will leave you and it will be virtually instantaneous after you release it from its deepest place inside of yourself.

> God will help you if you will ask Him.

Again, God will help you with this if you ask Him. But don't expect Him to do everything. You must proactively make yourself go through this process of letting it go, not just asking God to take it from you. There is a difference between expecting God to take it from you as you stand by and letting go from the depths of your soul. Your soul can be cleansed and God will come in and literally cleanse your soul.

C) Provide maintenance on yourself. Daily or weekly maintenance of your mind, emotions, spirit, and body is crucial to stay stable, healthy, and strong. In doing so you are capable and competent to maximize your God-given potential much better than you can when you are wounded and sickly.

A maintenance program can include prayer, worship, uplifting music, listening to CD's, watching DVD's, attending conferences, attending church, private meditation, personal reflection, reading books, counseling, positive friendships, fasting, eating healthy, exercising, recreation, fun, laughing, and alcohol and food consumption in moderation.

You don't have to use food to medicate your problems, because you will end up abusing it and potentially becoming addicted. Yes, it makes you feel good, but after a while the health problems of food, alcohol, and other substance abuse will create misery and unhealthiness in your life. It is better to address and heal the wounds and remove the associated pain rather than self-medicating.

Step #7: Create a new model

Establish a new pattern of thinking by design. Then decide to act on those new productive thoughts that produce the desired results in your life. Not just any results, but the ones you pre-design that produce life in you.

Always choose life in everything that you do, then practice these positive changes consistently and with determination until they become automatic in you. Automatic means that you won't have to make yourself say or do it anymore, but it will happen before you know it. It has to become the new "normal" in you. This will also prevent you from defaulting back into old thoughts, behaviors, and relationship patterns.

> **Denounce the old and receive the new.**

A very effective remodeling exercise is to imagine how you would act if you were no longer practicing the old unwanted, negative, or destructive behaviors but were instead practicing the new productive ones. Picture in your mind what it looks like acting it out. You should even write a list of your new thinking and behaviors so you can renew your mind to them on a daily basis. Place this list somewhere that is obvious to you (mirror, lamp stand, or refrigerator) so that you can see them every day.

It also helps to say you denounce the old and receive the new. You should be consciously aware of the old behaviors as well, so that if they prompt you, you can recognize them and not practice them. Remember, what fires, wires. Do not practice behaviors that you do not want to revive and fire up again.

It is furthermore important to "red flag" old negative behaviors so that you don't flow with them when they prompt you to act. Practice the new ones with aggression and consistency. Create separation between you and the old life as soon as you can. This is also accomplished by pre-programming your thinking, actions, and responses in advance, before you are prompted with the old ones again.

Step #8: Replace the old with the new

There are sequential steps that you can follow to remove old patterns and replace them with new ones. Here they are:

A) Recognize the old patterns.

B) Stop them and say "no" to them.

C) Invalidate them (no longer submit your will to them).

D) Don't practice, obey, believe, embrace, or be afraid of them.

E) Identify the new productive patterns to put in place of the old patterns.

F) Validate them (submit your will).

G) Practice the new ones until they are automatic. (It also helps to go into your memory and identify the wound's origination point, which is the first time it happened to you.)

H) Identify with the new behaviors as the new you and do not continue to say you still do those things or you are still that person. Instead, say you "used" to do them. They are now the old you.

Section IV

Restoring Your Health

In recent years, the Gallup polls found, most Americans define success and happiness as health. Consistently enough, the Bible also has something to say about that issue. Third John chapter two says "…I pray that you may prosper in every way and [that your body] may keep well, even as [I know] your soul keeps well and prospers." As a Licensed Therapist for many years, I have also found this issue of health to be the significant influencing factor in determining people's happiness in their lives. If you are sick physically, especially over long periods of time, it affects your happiness and can cause depression, anxiety, or panic. If you are emotionally wounded and remain in a state of emotional unhealthiness, it influences your level of happiness. If you have an unhealthy relationship, it will obviously affect your happiness and your own health. The point is that your health is a priority and must be maintained intentionally. Of course, maintaining your health also requires that you recognize when you are not healthy in any regard, and do something about it. Doing something about your health means that you go beyond being worried, concerned, and afraid, but that you identify where you are unhealthy and do what it takes to get healthy. Maintaining health does not happen accidentally. It is a purposeful effort.

Restoring your health also involves the restoring of your self-worth and self-image, which often requires that you reconstruct wounded parts that lower your self-perceptions and hinder you from seeing and pursuing your potential in life.

Chapter 8

Applying Love to Your Self-Image

Restoring health begins internally with a healthy self-worth and self-image, which is enabled by love. Health means that all of the individual parts of your "system" are functioning as intended and in their intended purposes. Health will create success on many levels. Wholeness is when all of the healthy parts are connected together so that the entire system is functioning in its intended purpose.

You can still function if some of the parts are not healthy. In fact, most people function that way every day of their lives. They do not function at their maximum potential or efficiency, but they function.

All health and wholeness begins internally and moves outward. If you are spiritually sick, it will affect your thinking, emotions, and even your physical health. One of the ways it affects your physical health is due to the act of self-medicating in order to cover pain. Prolonged medicating in the form of drug or alcohol abuse will eventually hurt your physical health.

Love God

Love originates from God Himself because God is love. Romans 13 says that the love of God meets all the requirements of the law relating to our fellow man. This means love meets all the requirements of a relationship with another person. Love will work in any interaction, relationship, self-esteem, and relationship with God.

Experiencing the love of God is the ultimate love-experience you could have. God is love and therefore if you love God, self, and others with God's love, you cannot go wrong.

As a counselor I have profoundly realized that the love of God (with God, for ourselves, and for other people) will cross all boundaries and all differences, regardless of backgrounds, race, color, beliefs, self-worth, image, past hurts, socio-economic status, church denomination, or appearances. Love meets all the requirements of the laws of life and behavior.

Scripture says to owe no man anything but to love him … love meets all the requirements of the law … love covers a multitude of sins … love casts out fear … God is love. When you don't know what else to do in a relationship, love (of God, self, and others) will be your healthy guideline and show you what to do spiritually, in self-development and protection, and in relationships. God's love will never abuse you or want you abused (self or from others) in any way.

Love yourself

When we love God and allow Him to love us, we can then apply love to ourselves. This is self-love. When you love yourself with God's love, you can healthily love others. If you do not love yourself, then you will not be properly equipped to love others.

Without God's love, we simply do not have enough fleshly or natural love in us to adequately love others. The fact is that we will never be good enough in our own power to love others. One of the reasons is because we are aware of our sins, imperfections, faults, shortcomings, mistakes, and secrets in life. We may also be aware of the sins and shortcomings of others. God's love empowers with the grace to love ourselves and others, even though we all have sinned.

When you value something, you protect and maximize it as an asset. Self-maintenance is applying God's love to your own self. When you maintain yourself, you will automatically want to develop your self-acceptance, self-worth, self-image, personal gifts, and personality strengths (more on gifts in Maximizing Potential section).

When you do not love yourself, you will experience self-condemnation, self-punishment, self-hate, and self-rejection. You will realize on some level that you may not feel worthy or valuable enough to stay healthy only for yourself. You may think others are worthy and you may even value yourself as long as someone else is valuing you. But as soon as you are in a position to see the value in yourself that can stand alone, you will treat yourself as less valuable and you will act accordingly.

Self-love means that you will develop and maintain your health in all ways. It also means that you will not be willing to hurt yourself. It should not be acceptable to hurt, abuse, or neglect something that is valuable. You would not throw a Rolex watch in the street and leave it there, but you might throw a one-dollar pen in the street because it is not as valuable.

> **Without God's love, we simply do not have enough fleshly or natural love in us to adequately love others.**

When you do not love yourself, you can allow self-hate, self-anger, self-rejection, and self-criticalness to hurt you. These destructive thoughts, emotions, and behaviors will be projected onto other people in the form of hate, anger, rejection, and criticalness. Whatever is in you, you will project onto others, especially in a time of prolonged stress. Whatever is in you will come out as the pressure increases. If you want to really know what is in you or in someone else, then observe them under stress.

Scripture says that godly sorrow produces repentance. The reason this is important to understand is that many people self-punish and condemn and have a lot of sorrow, but this type of sorrow is not godly sorrow. I call it earthly sorrow because it is carnal and not from God. This is why it does not produce repentance and therefore no positive change. If it were the God kind of sorrow, it would cause people to repent and change rather than their sorrow getting worse and bringing them into a state of darkness.

Self-love does not include arrogance, selfishness, pride, or criticalness. These negative characteristics are actually unhealthy and are often used as personal defense mechanisms so that others will not notice hidden insecurities. Self-love will not lack confidence. On the contrary, it will center a person's confidence and self-acceptance. Self-love will allow a healthy love for others.

If you love yourself, you can love others correctly and accept yourself and others as well. The love of God allows you to be worthy rather than unworthy to love and be loved.

The psychological and spiritual truth is that people act out in every behavior and in every relationship what they subconsciously think they deserve. It is a way that people measure whether or not they are accepted and whether or not they will accept others. Worthiness is negatively affected by past hurts, wounds, sins, and failures, whether self-inflicted or inflicted by some exterior source. This influences present decisions moving forward and generates internal messages and emotions, which create that internal measurement.

> **When you do not love yourself, you allow self-hate, self-anger, self-rejection, and self-criticalness to hurt you.**

The internal messages and emotions that create the worthiness measurement for self and others tells you what you do or do not qualify for regarding acceptance and whether you qualify for maximizing your potential in life.

Those who say, "This is the hand that was dealt to me," also believe that good things will happen to others but not to them. They believe in good things and in others' success, but subconsciously do not believe they themselves qualify. This is evidenced by people who act out self-hate by attacking their worth verbally or physically through self-mutilation (cutting and burning their body) as well as attempted or successful suicide.

When you apply God's love to yourself, you can then forgive yourself of your past sins and mistakes. Forgiving yourself means that you can release the debt you have held against yourself and release the self-punishment that comes along with unforgiveness.

Many of my clients through the years have been able to find a way to forgive others, but found themselves still unable to be free from the burden, anger, and torment of the past. When they genuinely forgave themselves and said they forgave themselves, they began to be free.

LOVE OTHERS

Matthew 10:27 says to "love the Lord your God with all your heart, with all your soul, with all your strength (body) and with your entire mind and your neighbor as yourself." Then Jesus told an attorney, "Do this and you will live."

What an amazing and serious statement made by Jesus Christ Himself! Love God, love yourself, and love your neighbor as yourself and you will live. We cannot ignore this truth. Love is for our benefit and for the benefit of others. When we are not renewed in God's kind of love, we will eventually become bitter and resentful, which will turn us into people we do not intend nor desire to be.

I do not think God's love is for the purpose of creating victims who cannot defend or speak for themselves. Love, on the contrary, replaces fear and timidity and provides the confidence to live a productive, healthy, and purposeful life. This kind of life includes healthy relationships.

When you love yourself, you can love others correctly.

As I said, with the hurts, offenses, disappointments, and wounds that occur in relationships, you need the love of God to empower you to heal, forgive, and speak the truth. Romans 13:8 says that "love fulfills all the requirements of the law." In the next verse it says that the greatest commandment is to "love your neighbor as yourself." When you love yourself, you will value, accept, and maintain your spirit, emotions, mind, and body.

Loving others will not be possible until you stop deciding if they deserve love. The fact is that many people do not deserve love or any other good thing they enjoy in life. People can be unthankful and even hateful and still have good things. Others have stolen, lied, cheated, and betrayed others to possess more things. Therefore they do not deserve good things, and certainly not love.

This kind of unresolved past offenses will hinder love because they are contrary to love. If they cannot love themselves, then they will not love others. And if they can't love others, then they cannot love themselves and cannot love God with God's love. The love they express will be a selfish love based upon acceptance, rules, and expectations.

Loving others does not mean that you place yourself in an abusive relationship with a destructive person. Love means you can love them and still draw boundaries proportionate to the level of their destructiveness. You do not owe them offense, hate, anger, or retaliation. You do owe them love. In doing so, you will remain healthy. Otherwise you will become contaminated with your own unresolved hate. After that, you will have inside of you the very thing you did not like about them. Hate will make you be someone you never thought you would be. It makes you unlovable in your behavior, and people then have to draw boundaries with you in order to protect themselves from the venom you spew out.

If you set your mind and attitude on this principle, it will keep you personally healthy and will keep your relationships healthy. When you don't know how to act with people who are angry, bitter, critical, or just unpleasant, just show love toward them. In most cases it will defuse and disarm them. People who are negative and unloving are negatively empowered by your negative response back to them, but they are defused when you do not get sucked up into their anger and problems. You can still show love without engaging them in conflict. You can stay away from their offenses and still show love.

This does not happen accidentally and cannot be left up to emotional impulse. You must pre-program this thinking into your mind and heart in advance, before you have the opportunity to try it. This kind of approach will also require God's help and you must ask Him to renew you in His love. Actually say this prayer: "God, I ask and I allow you to fill my heart with Your love and help me to show it."

When you ask God to get involved, He will, but you must submit your will to Him and allow Him to renew your heart with His love. When this happens, you will soften toward others and show more mercy. I have learned, as a counselor who meets daily with people with every problem and from every walk of life, that if you love them in spite of their faults and sins, you will be able to speak into their lives in a positive way. Let love do the work in them. Your part is to show it and God's part is to make love do its work.

Love is the approach, truth is the content

Love is the "approach" and truth is the "content." These are the two parts to communication.

Speaking in love does not require you to remove your truthful content, but it does require you to change your approach. People can hear the truth you are saying when you are more loving in the way you say it.

Do not get confused with truth and content. The two do not have to be expressed at the same level of emotional intensity in order for people to hear you and for you to speak clearly and effectively. Some people think that in order to be heard they have to be harsh, mean, and dominating or include personal attacks. Scripture says that a soft answer turns away wrath.

Soft does not mean timid and fearful. When you speak in love, you can soften the approach and still maintain the content of your message or purpose. For example, when a pilot is landing an airplane, the content of his knowledge about the plane and the landing procedures can be absolutely superior. But if his approach is too fast or too harsh, then the end result, regardless of his knowledge, can be destructive for him and others as well.

Similarly, your approach can determine if your content is heard and if it produces its intended results.

Self-worth

Self-worth is defined as the value and worth placed on self and the perceived value from others. It is the core value of a person.

According to Genesis 1:27, our self-worth (in His likeness) and self-image (in His image) was originally connected to God and not to other people's behavior toward us. Neither is self-worth or self-image dependent on other external influences.

Our true spiritual worth must not be attached to the acceptance or rejection of another person. It must be attached to God because we are created spirit beings, birthed from God in His image and likeness. He is our origination point and we must stay connected to Him as our source.

> **Your true spiritual worth must not be attached to the acceptance or rejection of another person.**

As we've discussed, self-worth is the amount of worth you place on yourself and the worth you believe other people place on you. It develops from birth as love and value are projected onto you. Your self-worth primarily develops from age 0-20 and your self-image primarily develops from ages 12-20 (depending on personality types and intellectual properties). This means that whatever happened in those years (good or bad) integrated into your worth and image and became your normal behavior.

However, because worth and image are developed, it means that you can develop and reprogram, by design, your self-worth and self-image into a healthy condition as an adult. But just because you can doesn't mean you will. This is why it is wise to get help.

Always remember, there is no shame in pursuing help. Despite any fears, pride, stubbornness, or strength, be open to the help that others can provide. Proverbs 11:14 say that there is safety in counseling.

SELF-IMAGE

Self-image is the way you view or see yourself and how you believe other people view or see you. It is your self-view.

Both self-worth and self-image are perceived first by your own reference points to your past behavior and experiences. Then you take on that identity and act that way because of your mental model of yourself. It becomes the norm.

There was a young girl who was told she was chubby growing up even though she was not. You know how adolescent and teenage girls can focus on one part of their waist or stomach and say they are chubby or fat, but they really are not. After several years of comments like this, she began to believe that she was fat and actually began to see herself that way and believed that everyone saw her that way. Eventually, she became overweight and accepted it as normal, even though she was not pleased with herself. As she got older, she only used her talents to the extent that she was assured that she would not be rejected because of her weight. This made her displeased and discouraged more with herself, but her "fat" image became her identity and ruled her decisions. If you looked at her pictures when she was young, you would say that she was not chubby or overweight at all. But because she developed that image and identity, she became it.

This is why people say words like "That's just the way I am," or "This is just me." They have developed an identity and accepted it. This is also how the "spirit of average" develops and integrates into our behavior because it becomes the model for our own worth and image. The self-worth (measure of worth) and self-image (self-view and perceived view from others) include the subconscious and unconscious measurements that feed the conscious thoughts and perceptions that promote and even drive average behaviors rather than the pursuit of our God-given potential.

The truth is, you will never maximize your potential, or even get a glimpse of it, if you do not believe you qualify. This is because of a pre-programmed and pre-conceived notion that trying to do so will always end in failure, confirming that you are not good enough, which will produce a disappointment that you are not willing to experience again.

I often hear people say, "It is better to not try than to fail." Furthermore, these same people explain that if others see them try and fail, then it is not just failure but also rejection. They simply don't want to be disappointed.

Nobody wants to be disappointed, but the reality is that they will feel the disappointment anyway on the inside. Then on top of that, they will revisit the disappointment periodically, and this is why they act negatively or destructively. They cannot love themselves and others because of the way they see themselves. They are aware of their low self-esteem and their eyes scan the behavior of others, looking for acceptance or rejection.

Believe that you qualify!

This hypersensitivity is why we see uncontrolled anger, rage, road rage, and various abusive behaviors. These are products of people who have low self-worth and who become enraged when others do not treat them as worthy or valuable. This is usually perceived, but can also be triggered by a real experience such as adultery, abandonment, or hurtful words that were spoken.

If you are hypersensitive, it's time to get healed.

Chapter 9

Do You Want Your Health Back?

An insecure person thinks that others act negatively toward them because the insecure person is unworthy and not valued. All behavior is interpreted through internal rejection filters.

That is why people mostly see themselves through the eyes of their own limitations and vulnerabilities regardless of what they look like on the outside and regardless of how positively others see them.

Positional self-image or self-view

Our self-image or self-view is the core image of ourselves at the core spirit level to our self-worth. This must not be attached to other people. Instead, it must be attached to God so that we can use our God-given gifts and personality strengths.

Positional image is fed by the self-worth and always corresponds with it. So if your self-worth is low, then your self-image will be low. You will then have to overcompensate in your situational image to feel better about yourself. When that happens, the external incoming interactions with people and things will determine your image and worth, which makes you dependent on the external to feel good about yourself. It also sets you up to have less or no worth, depending upon the acceptance or rejection of another person.

This position is contrary to the way God intended for your worth and image to function. He intended your worth to be connected to Him, the One who feeds your image and makes you stable and strong in your core self, regardless of another person's opinion or attitude about you.

SITUATIONAL SELF-IMAGE OR SELF-VIEW

The conditional and situational part of your image can be changed and modified (up or down) based upon your own productive or destructive choices, relationships, clothes, appearance, image, and other changing external factors. In addition, your perceived successes and failures in life and your level of development and acceptance from others, especially those you choose to be close to or imitate, will affect your self-image. You eventually become the product of what you have planted in your life.

Self-worth and self-image includes subconscious measurements and perceptions. Where you see it, doesn't always make sense:

- Logical/Illogical: Some people are born with physical and mental handicaps and they experience lower self-image ... while others with the same handicaps have a high self-image.

- Logical/Illogical: Some people have no real physical handicap (except the perceived one that they obsess over), yet have low self-worth and self-image because of bad experiences from their caregivers, parents, authority figures, and other relationships when they were children and in their developmental years.

- Illogical: Some people grow up in healthy environments and were trained and loved by healthy parents, yet they have low self-worth and self-image, not because they were victimized or neglected by someone else, but because of their own choices.

Destructive choices usually come from the false belief (from yourself or friends) that you are being treated like a child and you have no freedom. Then you might become critical of your loving parents and rebel against them. That rebellion breeds anger and resentment toward parents and possibly other authority figures, like God, and you abandon your closeness with those who love you, abandon your training, and abandon the morals you have learned.

This type of deception will promote destructive attractions and bad relationships, which usually result in behaviors that further damage your self-worth and self-image. The short of it is, your once healthy self-worth and self-image become damaged and are lowered due to self-inflicted pain and unnecessary scars. You will then have to overcome them when you decide to return to your good heritage and again become healthy and happy.

> **Your choices will dictate your overall health.**

Your choices will eventually dictate your overall health. If you have made decisions that produced unhealthy results, you must realize that you still possess the authority and power to make a change and get better results. There is hope! Better results happen by design, not by accident or default. There are specific steps you can take to improve and produce change (more in the Retraining the Mind section).

SUICIDE AND ITS EFFECTS

Sometimes people struggle with a dark cloud that seems to hang over them. The cloud may come and go, but it's always around.

This type of oppression and condition is more than just a low self-worth and low self-image. It is more serious and has to be dealt with on a spiritual, psychological, and a relationship level. Most often it includes treatment for chemical imbalance in the brain, which includes the balance of neurotransmitters.

This relentless dark cloud or heaviness can lead to anxiety, hopelessness, and depression. This ongoing misery, coupled with not being able to see a way out, can lead to suicide.

Suicide is more common that we want to think. There are many cases in my counseling practice where a family member (even a parent) commits suicide and it comes as a total shock to all family members and friends.

This act can never be erased and affects people in a lasting way. Not only is suicide a reflection of low self-worth, darkness, depression, and hopelessness, but it also represents thinking that is totally consumed with escape through death. The person is totally mesmerized with thoughts and feelings of death.

Suicide needs to be specifically mentioned because of its unhealthiness, and the negative effects it has on family, loved ones, friends, and even acquaintances. Research shows that suicide increases as hope decreases. Specifically, this applies to men over the age of 40 who are alone and feel they have been a failure and/or feel they have been betrayed, rejected, or abandoned by loved ones (more men commit suicide than women).

Suicide is one of the leading causes of death in the United States. We are talking about tens of thousands of people who commit suicide each year, and for every suicide, there were another 10 or 11 who tried. Suicide is a darkness that consumes the mind and emotions of people and they conclude there is no way out of the hopelessness and pain except through suicide.

Here are some of the ways that suicide negatively impacts others, especially family and loved ones, when a parent commits suicide:

> 1. It is a constant reminder to the children that their father or mother who was supposed to love them is no longer there, especially when they see other children with their parent.
>
> 2. Children also can begin to wonder if they are cursed in some way and they even develop a doubt or a fear that they will experience something or have thoughts or feelings in their life that would make them also commit suicide at some point.

3. Unlike divorce, the children can no longer speak to the parent who committed suicide.

4. Suicide can also allow the same spiritual oppression that was on the one who committed suicidal to torment other family members. The same "darkness" that oppressed the parent can oppress the child, especially if the child does not have a spiritual foundation or a parent who enables and empowers the child to make it through this uncertain and confusing time. If the father committed suicide, then the child often feels unprotected from potential intruders. There is a void of the father's God-given purpose, which was to protect (tend/guard) the family, both naturally and spiritually (Genesis 2:15).

5. Children can feel abandoned and not good enough for the remaining parent. Children can take on false responsibilities and personalize the fact that a parent left as "proof" that they did not do enough or were not valuable enough.

6. Children can feel guilty, as if they did something wrong that made the parent do this.

7. The children and loved ones have to experience the feeling of grief, confusion, and loss in addition to wondering why and how this traumatizing thing could have happened.

8. Family and loved ones search their memories and wonder if they should have, or could have, done something better to help or prevent the suicide, and they may even feel guilty over what they could have done to stop it.

9. Family and loved ones are placed in the position of unexpectedly selling their homes, cars, and anything that

reminds them of the trauma (especially if the suicide was in the home or a personal vehicle).

To create hope, you must confront the spiritual oppression aspect of any darkness. If you are oppressed, then your mind is bound, confused, obsessed, and tormented over what is bothering you and what you are afraid of. You want relief, but there is demonic activity around you that creates a cloud of heaviness, sadness, and depression over you and it tries to direct your mind to thoughts of death or suicide.

> **An integral part of being restored to health is freedom from oppression.**

Many people who have death thoughts do not have suicidal thoughts, meaning they do not intend to kill themselves and would never do so, but they do think about "not being here." In comparison, suicidal thoughts are about considering how they might commit suicide (gun, hanging, etc.).

An integral part of restoring to health is freedom from this oppression. If you are spiritually oppressed, then it is hard for you to tell the difference between spiritual oppression and a mental, emotional, or chemical problem.

This will help. A spiritual attack often comes suddenly and strongly. Proverbs 3:25 describes a spiritual attack by saying, "Do not be afraid of sudden terror (type of fear) nor of trouble from the wicked (the Amplified Bible uses the words 'sudden blast') when it comes."

In comparison, thought-induced emotions, troubles, and fears will always follow and correspond with thoughts pertaining to the troubled emotions. In order to change the emotions, the thoughts must be targeted aggressively and intensely and replaced with new ones that promote good emotions and feelings. It is also helpful to note that when you are overriding the negative thoughts, it is even more effective to use spoken words, especially Scripture confessions, to replace the old thoughts with new productive ones. This process must be aggressive, consistent, and prayerful. If you need deliverance from oppression or possession, seek out a minister or ministry that specifically focuses on deliverance from oppression.

Is there hope?

I am often asked as a counselor if there is any hope that a person who is unhealthy can really change permanently. This is usually asked in the midst of desperation and weariness.

Yes, health and wholeness can be attained and it begins internally and manifests itself outwardly. You cannot see yourself as a victim because if you do, then you will not take on your part of the responsibility to change. This will in turn place the responsibility on other people and circumstances. In life, there can always be an excuse and even a reason to place blame and responsibility on someone or something else. If you do not take charge of your life, then something or someone else will.

However, in this transformation process, you are responsible for your part and God is responsible for His part. You must be willing to do what it takes to get healthy. God will in turn, empower you with the people to help you, and He will empower you with His anointing to be free, healthy, and whole.

The difference between health and wholeness is that health is all about you and your separate parts being well, healthy, and functioning. Wholeness, on the other hand, is all of the parts working together synergistically. For example, all of your organs can be healthy, but all of them must work together and have a connection in order to have wholeness. The same scenario applies to your camera, computer, or car. Fully functioning parts fully functioning together — that is required for wholeness!

Good health is available for everyone, including you!

Good health is available for everyone, including you. It is not just for someone else. You must dare to step out and push through fear at the risk of failure, even if you do not feel that there is any hope.

Sometimes it will feel hopeless, especially after a lot of bad experiences, but that is why feelings are not always a good measuring tool for hope. Just create a new positive experience with your actions, step by step. When you have accomplished something positive that you previously thought to be too difficult, you will look back and wonder why you did not do it sooner!

A REAL EXAMPLE

Bill had obsessive/compulsive personality disorder. His parent's marriage was rocky all his life. There was lots of conflict, his dad was lenient, and Bill struggled with depression and insecurities. He was never trained by his father and they never "connected" as a father and son.

As Bill grew up, he withdrew and secluded himself. His dad wasn't a leader and his mom was critical, demanding, harsh, and not affectionate, and this destabilized Bill as a young man.

Both Bill and his father suffered from an obsessive compulsive disorder (OCD). "OCD" means that you follow excessive and unreasonable thoughts, ideas, impulses, detailed rituals, and order, in an attempt to be in control and "safe" from some type of perceived impending or potential danger. Interestingly, this is the one way that father and son would bond.

Bill was afraid of countless things, such as doorknobs, barcodes on anything, the scanner at a grocery store, opening mail, banks, germs, towels that touched the wall, and on and on it went.

When people have fears from bad experiences, more fears will come and they seem like they are true. If you don't resolve the issue related to the fear, you will overcompensate with these or other fear-based controls. As a natural result, you feel safer by controlling your environment or territory. Sadly, the fear takes over. It always does.

Things got progressively worse, for the fears led to fear-based comfort zones, which meant that Bill believed he was unsafe when he was uncomfortable with any unknown scenario he faced. To avoid or reduce feelings of being unsafe, he would obey the OCD demands and dictates. When he did, he was more comfortable. Of course this confined him to a very limited territory which was his room in his parent's home.

When Bill's father first came in, he was miserable, hopeless, desperate, and in despair because his son was suffering from OCD. During our first session, my receptionist called me with anxious voice, that the son of my client was down in the lobby. Bill was 30 years old, unshaven, sweaty, with messed up hair, and no pants, shoes, or shirt. He was standing there in his boxers.

I brought Bill up to the office where his dad was seated. Bill was scared to touch anything. He held his hands close to his body. From his elbows to his fingers, he was as white as paper from washing 150-300 times a day. He would take two-hour showers, and then rewash if he touched a curtain or door. He feared germs or dirt would get him. And if he touched a shampoo bottle wrongly, he would have to rewash. He would ask for a towel from someone else, and he put requirements on them.

As you can imagine, Bill couldn't manage his own life. He had to have his mother or father or brother or sister bring him towels, and the towels couldn't touch the walls. He was phobic of barcodes touching his body. He wouldn't let things with barcodes touch him. He thought he would get the "mark of the beast" and be eternally damned if he touched a barcode.

Bill received disability checks, but he wouldn't cash them. He thought that if he registered at the bank that the increased exposure would allow the government to track him. He would never cash his checks. At 30 years old, he had no driver's license … because that required a thumbprint.

The core fear was the fear of death. For others, there are eternal or physical or freedom or relationship or mobility fears, but Bill was afraid of eternal death the most. Mentally, he obsessed about it. He could hardly listen to any scripture or any moral principle because he thought he might think wrongly about it. He believed he had to think perfectly, so he couldn't go to church because he didn't want to mess up a verse or his understanding. Again, it confined him to his room in the house.

But Bill was brilliant. Many times, brilliant people develop "what if" scenarios. They consider every unsafe or dangerous scenario, and those thoughts induce fears. The fears then get programmed into their mind, nervous system, and body and they constantly try to fight it off with perfectionist rituals. It's a horrible bondage.

Many people think that those with disorders are ignorant people, but Bill had a photographic memory, which also played against him and his phobias. Three months (I counseled him for several years) into sessions with him, he was sitting across from my desk in a chair and we were taking a break. I picked up the office phone (a hand-held phone) and I turned and pushed the buttons … beep … beep … and I talked to wife and hung up.

A month later, at 11 p.m. at night, Bill called my wife at home asking for me. I happened to be out of town, and she asked how he got our number. He replied, "I memorized the number from hearing the beeps when he called you." This was three months later! He could also memorize confessions, and he memorized every word, period, and comma, on a full piece of paper, with no errors. Bill was brilliant.

People with wounds and struggles don't have to be crazy or ignorant. Rather, it is part of humanity for people to have wounds. That's just life. You can't escape it. We will have struggles and temptations and traumas. That's life. The message is, no matter how difficult the struggle, there is an answer if you are willing to get help, walk it out, and address the fears.

Today you would never recognize Bill. We worked spiritually and mentally and emotionally and physically through his issues. We talked about conflicts and things that started it all. There is hope for Bill, and there is hope for you. Time doesn't heal everything. You have to go to the problem, identify it, expose it, and then resolve it.

Chapter 10

Trauma Bonding and Relationships

When you are restoring your health, relationship health must also be considered a vital part of this process. You cannot totally restore your health, and permanently improve your life, while leaving destructive relationships in place.

In my practice, I have realized over the years that relationships either bless you or curse you. There is really nothing in between. Relationships will empower your positive change or empower your old lifestyle. Often your old friends will never change with you, but they will feel that you are abandoning them or leaving them when you are changing. They want you to stay in the old bond with them and this creates the same trauma and problem in your life, with the same negative influences, as it always has.

This changes things

When you change, your relationships have to change. If people want to change, they will change, but you cannot change them and are not their savior. There is one Savior and you are not that Savior. In fact, a Savior gets crucified for other people's sins, and the same will be true if you place yourself in that role. Many people have tried it throughout the centuries, but all have failed and all will always fail. You do not have the authority or the power to change the heart of another person. That transformation is between them and God.

People might temporarily change for you, but it is not permanent. This temporary change is only short-term behavior modification, and if they are doing it for you and not for themselves, then 100% of the time they will revert to their old established patterns. I guarantee the change won't last. They may even blame you for it in some way, but they will always go back to their old patterns until they are really ready to change out of their own desire and desperation. It will, at that point, be their own decision.

> Evidence of change is called "fruit." Without it, nothing has changed.

Sometimes a crisis gets people's attention and wakes them up, and sometimes it does not. But one thing is for sure, and that is, you will find out sooner or later, any change will be evident by their long-term behavior, which is called fruit. You will fully recognize and fully know people by their fruit, not by their convincing words and not by their sincerity.

Bearing fruit takes time and requires a process of having vision, cultivating ground, planting seed, watering the seed, measuring results, and benefiting from those results. By the time you go through that process, the fruit of change will be obvious and evidenced by your new beliefs and consistent actions. This change can be confirmed over a minimum of six months and not before. During that time period, you must work on your change aggressively and allow other competent people to assist you.

No one can accomplish this type of change all alone. Do not isolate yourself or try it alone, for trying to improve alone is a manifestation of fear or pride and neither of those mechanisms will help you improve. Instead, they will help you stay stuck where you are. Additionally, doing it alone will take you longer and the results will be deficient in some way.

Relationships hurt or help

In therapy, I hear every story known to the human mind and I hear about every possible relationship scenario, and in the final analysis it will always be true: relationships are a blessing or a curse depending on each party's health (or lack of it) and the purpose for the relationship.

Understanding the purpose for relationships is crucial. Purpose means the "why" or the reason for the existence for anything. The reason for the relationship can be healthy or unhealthy. For example, unhealthy purposes for a relationship would include:

- they drink well together,
- she looks good in tight jeans,
- they have the same wounds, traumas, or addictions in life,
- one pursued the other, who finally gave in, or
- one has problems and the other is going to try to change or improve him or her.

Without question, you want relationships that will be healthy and beneficial to you. The productive purpose for relationships include spiritual, personality, beliefs, and goal compatibility. Most relationship problems start out with personal problems that are acted out on each other in the relationship until the relationship is damaged. Sometimes both people in the relationship are wounded and other times just one person is primarily wounded and acts it out in the relationship.

TRAUMA BONDING

Earlier, I explained that "Trauma Bonding" was looking back in your memory for the sole purpose of reinforcing your bad experience because it causes you to live in the past and to bond with the past.

I will now expand Trauma Bonding to be this: experiencing a trauma in life (abuse, molestation, betrayal of adultery, neglect, cruelty, abandonment of a parent, etc.) and then repeating it in some way. This includes you repeating the trauma or someone else repeating that same trauma back to you.

Trauma Bonding happens all the time in relationships. Usually when a person gets involved in a relationship in order to improve, rescue, save, or help someone who is wounded in some way or has problems.

A relationship like this will always, immediately or eventually, end up in some kind of trauma. This is mainly because God did not create one person to have the power or authority to change another person permanently. Always remember this principal truth that I have learned as a Therapist who counsels approximately 7-10 hours per day: You must not desire and strive for someone else's improvement more than you desire it for yourself.

But this reality doesn't stop people from trying.

#1 — The Savior Syndrome

If saving someone from his or her problems is your primary motivator (conscious or subconscious) for getting involved in a personal relationship, then you are trying to be that person's savior. Don't do it. Trauma will be the result!

This is especially common for women who get involved in relationships with men to save, change, help, improve, or turn a "bad boy into a good boy." It never works!

> "I thought I could turn a bad boy into a good boy."
> — *Anonymous girl in therapy*

Subsequently, when the man does not improve, the woman feels that she is not good enough. This in turn lowers her self-worth and self-esteem to a deeper level for, she reasons, she was not good enough to change him.

But she doesn't quit. She keeps trying! She tells him how much he has hurt her, and when he shows some sympathy for her tears, she feels a false hope that he is changing ... and she continues her quest to rescue and change him for another prolonged period of time. Without question, she is in denial to believe that he will eventually change for her.

If you are involved in a relationship like this, recognize that you are in the middle of Trauma Bonding, and it is going to prevent you from finding a better spouse. Additionally, the Trauma Bonding can cause you not to be attracted to a quality person you would really prefer, all because you fear rejection. If that isn't enough, the Trauma Bonding enslaves you to the false responsibility of being the one who does not abandon the needy person like everyone else has (perhaps there was a good reason for it!).

You are not, and cannot be, the savior to anyone.

#2 — Repeating traumas

When a person has been traumatized in the form of molestation, abuse, parent's divorce, absentee father/mother, addictions, anger/rage, etc., they repeat that same behavior in some way and usually act it out on someone else. They usually victimize someone else (like they were victimized) rather than just victimizing themselves. These other victims or allies to the trauma, repeat the trauma to the next generation, and the "generational curse" continues.

Trauma can also come in the form of some seemingly innocent or non-important ways, such as laziness, lying, minimizing potential, etc. These behaviors, when acted out in front of children, spouses, and others, will create a problem which will turn into a trauma in later years. Children will repeat the behavior that was modeled for them.

> **You must not desire and strive for someone else's improvement more than you desire it for yourself.**

Laziness and bad work ethic are two notorious behaviors that will have a long-term negative impact. Scripture says that poverty will come quickly to a lazy man. Laziness hides behind a cloak of excuses, and the lazy person becomes the "victim" of everything. Some of the common excuses that the lazy person uses include:

- "I don't feel good."
- "I didn't get enough sleep."
- "I have a sore throat."

- "The alarm didn't go off."
- "They didn't like me."
- "There are no jobs left."
- "The economy."
- "I'm overqualified."
- "It's not a good career move to take that job."
- "I've applied everywhere."
- "I'm not 'ready' to get a job."
- "It doesn't pay enough."
- "I'm too busy."
- "If I work I'll lose my unemployment."

Laziness is just one example. Whatever the trauma, it will repeat. The molested can molest, the liars can lie, the abused can abuse, the abandoned can abandon, the neglected can neglect, the rejected can reject, the degraded can feel degraded, the unworthy can act unworthy, and the not good enough can act not good enough.

All of these types of traumas and wounds will:

A) Cause the trauma to repeat itself in the next generation of children or in the spouse.

B) Will guarantee that the traumatized person will never repeat the same trauma.

Which will it be for you? If you have been traumatized, then you know how it feels. Have no tolerance for trauma at all!

#3 — Sabotaging Techniques

In a relationship, the person with the trauma background usually creates unnecessary traumas, problems, and conflicts in order to bond or to get close. This is familiar territory, so further trauma is not only normal, it is needed.

Unfortunately, this kind of bonding creates so many ongoing problems that any closeness in the relationship is sabotaged with the constant problems. It's a no-win proposition.

#4 — Negative Attention

Negative attention is created to deal with the trauma or problems. This is no way to establish a lasting relationship, but it is what a trauma-bonded person knows and expects.

#5 — Common Pain, Problems, or Addictions

Bonding can also occur through common addictions or past traumas, such as drinking, abuse, drugs, lifestyles, angers, hurts, etc. The saying, "Birds of a feather flock together," certainly applies when it comes to trauma.

#6 — Negative Attractions

Negatives attract when trauma is involved. This is happening if you find yourself getting involved in relationships with people who suffered from or still possess the same problems that you experienced.

This is why people who had an alcoholic mother or father will often marry an alcoholic. It doesn't seem to make sense, but due to trauma bonding, the negatives attract.

JUST SAY "NO!"

You will never be able to make/force people to change permanently. They must desire it for themselves or be desperate enough to change because they no longer want the pain, or they want something better.

If you try, it will produce codependency, frustration, anger, feelings of not being good enough, and failure. In the end, they will not change … but you will, for the worse!

When people say they do not deserve you or they use any similar phrase, they are actually trying to warn you that they will act unworthy and undeserving at some point. They recognize that they are not compatible and are not good enough for you. This is not a statement or attitude of humility, it is a warning!

Remember that most people are not motivated by desire and vision, but rather by pain, crisis, and fear. If you want to know how motivated people are to change, watch their behavior under the threat of forced change!

> **You do not need trauma in your life. None at all!**

For example, I saw one man facing divorce if he didn't work on his marriage. He showed a willingness to change as long as there was hope for reconciliation, but as soon as there was evidence that the marriage was over, he instantly reverted back to his old negative or destructive behaviors. It showed that he did not truly desire change. (Sadly, for him, the cycle will continue; someone will take him in, then grow tired of his behavior, and he'll move to the next relationship. He is trauma bound, but isn't willing to change.) If he had really wanted to change, he would have continued to work on his marriage until things did change.

Simply put, do not put yourself in a compromising situation. Say "NO!" to any Trauma Bonding. You don't need it.

CHAPTER 11

OVERCOMING FEARS

Fear is a thought and feeling of hidden or impending danger that creates a sense of being unsafe, exposed, or vulnerable. In order to be restored to health, each and every one of your fears must be recognized, labeled correctly, and dismantled. The actual fear messages need to be broken down.

Fears are interesting, for they have internal messages that speak to the mind and promote the fears and the impending danger feelings associated with the fears. Breaking down the fear messages will produce freedom from validation of those fears.

FROM BAD TO WORSE

Most people don't realize it, but when they bring in control mechanisms to handle their fears, they end up making matters worse. The three most common fears are:

1. **Fear of being controlled** (controlled = dominated, planned, manipulated, mastered, confined, trapped, limited, suppressed by someone or something else, predictable, constraints, obsessing)

2. **Fear of not being in control** (not in control = immature, can't restrain/constrain, rogue, disobedient, outside of established boundaries)

3. **Fear of being out of control** (out of control = a behavior void of boundaries, unpredictable, erratic, undefined, destructive, unstable)

Control mechanisms to control these fears do not really protect people from what they are afraid of, but rather it breeds and projects into the people the very fears that control them. The same walls and control mechanisms that people use to protect themselves (falsely) from perceived outside dangers (people, closeness, hurt, intimacy, etc.), are the same walls that keep the fears and unresolved problems bottled up inside of them.

That is why control mechanisms are unhealthy and will eventually control you and put you in its box, as we've already discussed. The desire to feel in control and not out of control or being controlled, will drive you into an increasingly narrow space. Eventually, you will be completely convinced (because of your emotions and bodily feelings) that the controls are actually protecting you from what you are afraid of. When you are afraid or anxious, you will narrow your boundaries until you feel comfortable again.

> **When you break out of your box, you will feel uncomfortable.**

Sadly, your comfort zones are actually molding your behavior into conforming to the fear-based controls. You end up obeying the controllers that you established to protect you in the first place. For example, suppose you feel unsafe about driving on certain roads, so you obey the control fears and decide not to drive on those roads. You have just further empowered the control fears.

It is a deception because controlling does temporarily (only) reduce your anxiety and the fears that create your anxiety. This is why it's so easy to think you are protected with your control fears, but eventually and inevitably the controls will take control.

Do you really want to break out of the box?

When you break out of the box, you will feel uncomfortable. The confines and dictates of the box feel more comfortable because you are used to them. You feel comfortable right where you are. Will you break free?

Some people believe that staying in the box, regardless of how small it might be, will actually protect them from what they fear. They don't realize that their control mechanisms are going to feel violated and they will usually feel exposed, unsafe, and unprotected if they push back. But just because the feelings are there doesn't mean that it is true! They need to break free of the box, but doing so is going to wreak havoc on their control mechanisms.

The controls are, after all, only perceptions and they do not actually protect you from true impending or unknown dangers and certainly do not make you safer. These type of controls are consciously or subconsciously producing a "sense" or feeling of security and safeness in you. This feeling is a false measurement, but it nonetheless makes you feel safe.

However, there is a difference between true safety and a feeling of safety and security. You should not always believe what your feelings tell you. Feelings are real and often very powerful, but they are not the truth. You measure the truth by results, not by feeling. Feeling motivation is a deceptive measurement for security. Productive decisions are decisions made out of knowledge, wisdom, understanding, and discretion, not fear.

When you feel that you are not in control, out of control, or being controlled, then you will typically begin to control more in order to compensate because of the discomfort and anxiety it produces. The truth is that this fear-based type of control is indeed fear driven.

> **Every fear will lie to you. That's what fears do.**

As I have stated, you are not actually safer just because you depend on these types of controls and comfort zones. These mental or ritualistic control mechanisms do create comforts and discomforts, but they have no real power to actually protect you from any true unknown or impending dangers that create fear, worry, or concern in you.

The fear is lying to you. It tells you that control is protecting you and you are safe within the box, but that is not true. You do not control fear and its dictates and demands. Fear eventually dictates behavior and then demands that you obey it.

WITHSTANDING THE PRESSURE

If you are serious about getting out of the box, recognize that the pressure is going to increase. Every fear-based control is going to prompt you if you dare stray outside of its parameters. The comfort zones that are created, as you become conditioned to feel comfortable when you obey and conform to the box, are going to try to push you back into the box.

It will be uncomfortable! In essence, you've been trained to obey the box by the way you feel. These feelings can be generated in your emotions, your body, or your nervous system. These feelings are very powerful and can graduate to anxiety and then panic, which can then produce anxiety and panic disorders that put an extreme amount of stress on your mind, nerves, and body. It is even possible that an acute or chronic stress disorder could develop.

When people have recurring experiences, they end up believing those experiences, even if the experiences are driven by unhealthy thinking and behaviors. People do eventually believe their own experiences. The problem is that an experience that is birthed and driven by destructive thinking can make people believe a lie.

The lie in this case is that you are safe only if you stay in that box. The truth is that fear always lies and always ends up controlling you. This is a horrible bondage that creates torment. Fear has torment (I John 4:18 KJV). Torment starts in the mind and then expands and manifests in the nerves and the body.

As you may know, torment is stressful and you cannot control torment. The answer is to no longer believe that the fear is telling you the truth. Fear is not your ally or your protector. You must tap into your belief system and remove that false belief.

WALKING FREE!

When you no longer believe that fear makes you safer, then that change in your belief will relinquish fear's power and validation in you. In place of the old belief, you must insert (by design) a new belief, a belief that states that fear-based controls no longer protect you and the feelings, sensations, and discomforts you feel now are only temporary and are not a true indication that you are exposed to some type of danger.

During the transition of changing your beliefs and behaviors, you will experience discomfort on some level. But remember, these discomforts are not telling you the truth. The answer is not in trying to control, fight, or suppress the old fear thoughts and promptings. The answer is in changing your thoughts and beliefs about the fear.

The fear messages will still speak to you, but when they do, just recognize them for what they are (just an old program) and let them pass on by. Then you don't have to be afraid of those old thoughts any more because you have a new revelation of what they are. As a result, you become more and more separated from them. This new experience of separation will teach and condition you that the fear messages and comfort zones were all a lie, and that you are empowered to separate from all old programmed ways of thinking, and experience permanent relief in your nerves and body. Relief at last!

> **Believe that fear is no longer telling you the truth.**

If you continue in the fear-based behaviors, you will continue to be confined in a symptomatic prison. You will not want to violate the box because you don't want to experience the related feelings of discomfort. If you live by fear you will be ruled by fear. "You are a slave to whatever controls you," says 2 Peter 2:19. This is the greatest problem with fear-based controls ... you think you are in control and they are controlling you!

As I have said, when you try to get out of your box, then you will feel uncomfortable and interpret that feeling as true danger and you will want to conform to the fear and get back in the box. Resist the urge. Resist the lie. Stay free!

THE FRUIT OF FREEDOM

I am often asked what the difference is between self-control and fear-based controls. The answer is in the fruit.

Fear-based controls start out feeling good but will, in the end, create anxiety or even torment if you violate them. In addition, you will live in the confines of a box that minimizes your potential and activities and enjoyment of life. That is not fruit you want to eat, much less produce out of your life.

> You can walk free!

Self-control does not create fear or anxiety if you do not obey it. Instead, self-control will provide true goals and boundaries (do's and don'ts) in your behavior that will keep you on a straight path to maximize your potential and gifts.

In summary, self-control is self-discipline, while a fear-based control mechanism is pain, anxiety, torment, and control … of you.

HEALTHY DECISION MAKING

There are five mechanisms to making quality decisions that will guide and protect you and insure good results. These five mechanisms are productive and are not based in fear. They will also help you accurately measure true risk, liabilities, and dangers and will produce the results you want in your life. What's more, they will produce a healthy belief system upon which you will think and act.

These five elements are knowledge, wisdom, understanding, discretion, and discernment. I define them as follows:

#1 — Knowledge

Knowledge is the "what" of any information, such as knowing what to do in any given situation, knowing what you want, or having knowledge of a concept, goal, or vision for the future. *Webster New American Dictionary* defines knowledge as; 1. Understanding gained by actual experience 2. Range of information 3. Clear perception of truth 4. Something learned and kept in the mind.

When you know what to do in any given situation, you have vision you can build upon. However, you can know what you want to achieve in the next six months, but must also know how to attain it.

#2 — *Wisdom*

Wisdom is the "how" of any information. It is how you attain or reach a goal, how to use the knowledge you have (You can possess a gun, but if you do not know how to use it, the knowledge doesn't help you and can even be destructive to you as well as others.), and insight and good judgment regarding what to do and how to do it.

Therefore, wisdom involves both knowledge and wisdom. Wisdom knows how to use the knowledge it has with sound judgment. Wisdom has special insight into how to think, act, and respond. Consider these:

- "Do not forsake wisdom, and she will protect you." (Proverbs 4:6)

- "I wisdom, dwell together with prudence; I possess knowledge and discretion." (Proverbs 8:12)

- "For through wisdom your days will be many." (Proverbs 9:11)

Found in Proverbs and in the first few verses of Ecclesiastes, the following words and phrases are used in association with wisdom: words of insight, years added, fools despise wisdom and instruction, reward, discerning, stores up commands within you, the principal thing, understanding, fruit, humility, take advice, lips of the wise, prudent, give thought to their ways, instruction, fear of the Lord, insight, a rushing stream, patience, loves life, paying attention, a house built, like honey, future hope, kept safe, joy to his father, blessed, study, explore, increase.

These examples do not include all of the associations to wisdom, but as we look at these associations, we can grasp some of the definitions, applications, and benefits of wisdom.

#3 — Understanding

Understanding is the "why" of any information. It is the purpose, reason, or meaning of something. For example, the purpose for a pair of scissors is to cut with precision.

#4 — Discretion

Discretion is the "when" or "where" of any information. It is the timing and the place. "Discretion will protect you, and understanding will guard you," it says in Proverbs 2:11.

#5 — Discernment

Discernment is knowing the difference between right and wrong, black and white.

I happen to know that these five mechanisms will indeed guide and protect you and insure good results. They will help you accurately measure true risk, liabilities, and dangers and they will produce the results you want in your life. They will! I've seen it hundreds of times.

The choice is yours.

Section V

Setting Your Mind in Order

Your mind is a powerful thing and you must develop it and use it for a productive purpose. However, you do have the power to use it for a destructive purpose and it can take you to very bad places left unbridled and untrained. Every person has mental strengths and weaknesses. You must understand both so that you operate in your strengths and not your weaknesses and know the difference. Your mind connects with your emotions, your behavior, and your spirit. Consequently the way you think will make you healthy or unhealthy. So you must concentrate on the way you think as it relates to any unwanted, negative, or destructive behavior that you practice, involuntarily or not. Then realize that in order to change and correct those unwanted behaviors and patterns in you, you must find the thinking that is behind it and change that thinking and replace it with new, better thinking. If your ways are destructive, then there is destructive thinking behind it. If your ways are productive, then there is productive thinking behind it.

Also realize that it is possible to be destructive or negative in one (or some) areas and productive in others. It does not mean that you are all destructive or that you are a "bad person." Identify the behavior in yourself you desire to improve and work on that part of your life until change takes effect.

Chapter 12

Retraining Your Mind

Retraining your mind means that you retrain the way you think so that you don't repeat old patterns. Removing old patterns and replacing them with new thinking patterns is essential in changing your mindset and the way you make decisions. Changing your thinking changes the outcome so that you won't self-inflict the same old problems in your life that put you right where you really don't want to be.

However, in order to omit the same consequences in your life, you must change the way you believe, process information, and see yourself. Just because you have always done it one way doesn't mean that that is the best way or the most productive way. Repeating the same problematic thinking patterns over and over will always produce the same negative results.

> **Poverty and riches are products of thought.**

Identify the thinking that you bond with, justify, and even protect, and be serious enough to separate yourself from that thinking. Many times pride will interfere and prevent you from changing, even if you know you should change and agree on what should change in you. Let go of that pride or the old vow you made that keeps you bound and stuck in the same old place of hurt, hate, offense, anger, and resentment. Those emotions are powerful, but they won't protect you and they are not your allies.

In fact, they will eventually turn you into someone you don't want to be, and then they will destroy you.

You can reprogram your mind

Retraining or reprogramming your mind starts with the thought world, which means that as you change your thoughts, so you change your world. You can do it!

Thoughts are powerful, creative, and influential, and they eventually establish and reinforce your beliefs. The reason is that you will believe your own thoughts more than other people's thoughts and words. Additionally, your own thoughts are the first thoughts you hear and your own words are the words you hear first through your inner ear when you begin to speak.

God created the mind to learn and to influence your behavior. If you want to change behavior, you must first start with the thinking that promotes, directs, or justifies that behavior. If you modify behavior without permanently adjusting the thoughts, which include the beliefs behind that behavior, then you will only create short-term behavior modification rather than permanent change.

In order to experience new results in any given area of your life, old thoughts that produced unwanted, negative, or destructive results must be replaced. It is impossible to remain destructive in your thoughts and expect to be a productive individual. It's simply not going to happen.

The mind is where it's at

Your mind is where your thought activity interfaces with the rest of your system. It is the changing of your mind that changes you, because by changing your thoughts you change your beliefs, and with different beliefs, you will get different results.

Beliefs must be changed because people act out what they believe, even if that belief is irrational, negative, or destructive. Changing beliefs by design is the way beliefs are changed. Beliefs are not productively changed by waiting on some exterior force or experience to cause change. Unfortunately, this is how many unhealthy

SECTION V: SETTING YOUR MIND IN ORDER

beliefs are formed — as the result of an unhealthy experience, mistake, trauma, etc.

Those who believe "the only way you learn is by making mistakes" are the ones who do not change their beliefs by design. They are the ones who let things happen to them, and the results are not good.

When you make mistakes or suffer negative consequences from bad decisions (whether it was a mistake or not), you must realize that and learn from it ... so that you don't repeat the same old decisions that produced bad results.

> **You act out what you believe.**

Another great way to learn is to submit yourself to instruction, training, and learning from people who know more than you do on a given topic. It is not always necessary to go through life in pain or thinking that pain is the only teacher. This type of learning style typically results in unnecessary destructive living, lowering of self-worth, self-image, and self-esteem, and a distorted identity.

These emotional wounds and scars could create so much damage that you spend more time repairing yourself than you do maximizing your potential, gifts, and strengths. In fact, I often counsel with clients who, when asked to identify their gifts, have no answer and cannot access that information about themselves because it is an undeveloped area of their lives and unfamiliar territory. What a shame!

At this point I want to remind you of the three levels in the mind where thought activity occurs:

1. **Conscious:** Surface thoughts that operate in the present tense, real time (video analogy), with cognitive awareness of the mind.

2. **Subconscious:** Underlying thoughts that are just below the surface that are habitual and provide support and justification for conscious thoughts.

3. Unconscious: This is a backdrop/panoramic view or perspective of the world, self, others, and character that is automatic (something we think, say, or do without conscious or supporting beliefs, referenced, or premeditated thought at the time of the behavior).

All mental activity is generated within what I call the Arenas of the Mind. I label and group mental activity this way so that you can identify and access your own thoughts in order to remove the unwanted thoughts and intentionally replace them with thoughts that are purposefully designed in advance to produce certain desired results.

SEARCH AND DESTROY

It is much like a SWAT team that knows several suspects are hiding somewhere in a building. They cannot extract those suspects without a lot of searching, but if they know the specific room where the suspects are located, it won't be long before the suspects are captured.

> **The Law of Sowing and Reaping ... was designed to work in your favor!**

Thoughts that we want to remove and retrain are much the same. When we know in what arena an unwanted thought is located and where to insert the new one, we can, like the SWAT team, move in and extract the offensive thoughts.

Having this kind of understanding about your thought patterns will empower you to accurately monitor your own thoughts and change them by targeting specific arenas where thought activity is generated. In doing so, the behavior that is caused by those thoughts will be changed.

This is true because thoughts produce behavior and thought patterns produce behavior patterns. A pattern or pathway develops because of similar repetitive thoughts being carved out by repeated practice. This is one essential reason why thoughts must be targeted and changed in order to eventually develop new automatic behaviors.

By the time thoughts are automatic, the patterns are established and engrained into the subconscious and unconscious mind. The intent is to pre-design productive thoughts that will produce corresponding behaviors in the future, insert those productive thoughts into the mind, and purposefully practice them so they will become automatic behavior.

This process is founded on both scientific and spiritual principles. The scientific principle is based upon activity-depended gene expression and neurological pathways in the brain that send signals through the central nervous system to organs and then to the body, which creates muscle memory.

The spiritual (Biblical) principle is what I call the Law of Sowing and Reaping. I call it a law because all seed produces fruit. In fact, it is impossible for fruit to exist without corresponding seed. Even though this law is also scientific, because it governs every tangible man-made thing that exists, and it is the law that governs the soil and all reproduction with humans and living creatures, it is a spiritual law first. It is spiritual first because it originated from God Himself and became physical and living. This means that we can physically use it to benefit ourselves when we understand it.

Of course, it can also hurt us if we misuse these laws. Electricity provides power for lights, cars, and homes, but it can kill you if you put your finger in an electrical socket. Everything that we manage can be used for good or for bad, depending on the purpose. Everything that exists in the tangible originated out of the spiritual realm.

You can manage your own thoughts

You must be equipped with the knowledge to manage your own thoughts so that you can manage your life and make quality choices. Think about it. If you manage your own thought world, you can manage your own beliefs, will, memories, personality, intellect, self-image, self-worth, desires, imaginations, and conscience.

You can manage everything about you:

- **Your beliefs** by deciding what you receive as truth.

- **Your will** by deciding what you are willing and not willing to do.
- **Your memories** by using them as a reference point to improve and not repeat the same stupid decisions of your past.
- **Your personality** by operating in your strengths rather than your weaknesses.
- **Your intellect** by developing your gifts and potential to bless yourself and others.
- **Your self-image** by seeing yourself as created in God's own image and acting like it instead of operating in a fear of rejection.
- **Your self-worth** by loving God, yourself, and others.
- **Your desires** by knowing your desires and pursuing them with passion to reach your vision and goals in life.
- **Your imagination** by having vision for your potential and your future because the Scripture says that without vision people perish, which leads into discouragement, lack of purpose, mediocrity, failure, self-doubt, depression, and lack of fulfillment.
- **Your conscience** by keeping it clear and clean instead of it being depraved, desensitized, and unrepentant.

A REAL EXAMPLE

John, now a middle-aged man, always pursued and longed for the respect and appreciation of his father. He sought after it and it was his primary goal when he was younger and as he grew up. He also wanted desperately to help his father succeed in every way.

But John was rejected over and over by his father, who did not show affection, who never said, "I love you," and who didn't do things with him. This created a rejection and a belief that John wasn't valuable. To remedy that, John spent his life validating himself by fixing other people's problems. He would make them successful at his own expense, whether it was his money, time, or marriage.

He began to seek out appreciation from women (because his dad rejected him) and began to have sex with them. He wasn't going to open up to get hurt, but he still wanted to be close, so he would have sex but with no commitments.

This gave him a false sense of self-worth and self-esteem. Prostitutes were the perfect scenario for it simulated intimacy but required no commitment. However, John would overcompensate. When the prostitutes gave false compliments toward John (he craved appreciation), he started giving them things, such as money, cars, and even college expenses, all to make the prostitutes appreciate him more. All of this was at his own expense, and it almost ruined him financially.

John was a believer and a Sunday school teacher. The shame and guilt of his sexual addiction made him hide his issues, and he kept his secret world going. His professional life required him to travel, so that was a perfect cover for his addiction. He would teach in church, feel guilty, not want to do it any longer, but the secrecy kept going. Secrecy is one of the greatest enablers of any deviant behavior.

Eventually, John got married ... and he never told his wife. He kept his secret life of shame and addiction going. He was making a lot of money, but a lot of his money was going to these girls all over the country. He was paying money to get the appreciation he desired.

At home, John's rejection complex began to surface. His wife was affectionate, and that seemed good, but he became hyper-sensitive to her behavior if she didn't appreciate him as much as he felt she should. He stopped using prostitutes for a while, but after his wife wasn't meeting his needs, he went back, spending his money (and his wife's money) on prostitutes.

Eventually, his wife found out. His entire secret world of sex and prostitutes was opened up, and amazingly, his wife didn't want to divorce. She wanted to reconcile, but she began to hear comments from him that he knew "what good sex is" and she began to wonder if he was using her body. Naturally, she withdrew from him sexually, verbally, and emotionally. She lost respect for him, but she wanted to stay married because she loved him. She struggled with the wounds of betrayal and disappointment.

Whenever she withheld from him in any way, he would feel rejected and hurt (as with his dad), and he would withdraw from her. His "out" was to go back to sex and his secret life, which he did. It was at this point in their marriage that they came in for therapy.

Once John opened up and confessed things, they could heal things on the present tense level. They couldn't go back and stop the past, but they could establish and change things in the now. It was an addiction and a marriage issue, and a recovery issue.

John had to restore and correct his self-image. Rather than him functioning in a perceived self-image where he wasn't valued or where he needed sex elsewhere or where his wife wasn't valuing him, he needed to learn how his self-image was related to his actions. He had to retrain how he thought and to retrain his functions so that he could use his God-given giftings rather than getting attention, value, and appreciation through sex.

Time does not heal all things. You have to uncover the brutal truths and wounds, confess them so you can be healed down into the depths of those wounds. Then it's an exemplification of resolve, restore, and retrain. You have to resolve your past, restore your self-image so you can accept and love yourself correctly, and then retrain the way you think and act. Replace the old patterns with new ones. It's all on a spiritual and mental and emotional and physical level.

For John and his wife, their wounds were affecting them on all levels, but they have committed to working it out, and they are doing so.

THE STRUGGLE DURING THE TRANSITION

There is always a struggle during the transitional stage of any change. During this transitional shift from one place to another, your old programmed patterns will fight you and create discomfort because you are creating new neurological pathways and violating your old ones.

The old patterns dictated your level of comfort when you operated in the old patterns. Because of that, you are naturally familiar with the old patterns. They are known behaviors for you, but even if they are bad, they still have comfort zones, because familiarity creates comfort within that zone. So when you violate an old comfort zone (because you are trying to change for the better), you are going to feel uncomfortable.

At this point you must remember that just because you are uncomfortable does not mean that you are doing something wrong. Yes, discomfort does mean that you are violating an established boundary or operating outside your norm, but if your norm for that specific behavior is negative or destructive, then in order to change it, you will have to feel discomfort and violate that norm.

During the transition, it will be a struggle on several fronts:

- Your norms will be violated.

- You will have insecurities because of unfamiliarity and unknowns (this creates fear of the unknown or feelings and internal messages of being unsafe, unprotected, or impending danger).

- Your self-image and identity, which may be integrated and wrapped around the old behaviors, will feel a sense of loss as you separate from your old you.

- Your friends will also go through a transition because you are changing.

- Your feelings will change (do not measure your progress by your feelings) and will typically become unstable and unpredictable. Your feelings are tied to your old patterns and therefore your feelings will, for a while, try to pull you back into the old patterns.

These are not all of the ways that you and others will struggle during the transition of change. Again, even if the old patterns are destructive and a hindrance to your potential in life, it will still be a struggle on some level during your transition toward what is good, productive, and beneficial.

It is often hard to not slip back into old habits (because the old behavior is so automatic), so you must be aggressive, passionate, or desperate about staying with your new ways.

However, when and if you do slip back, just come out of the old pattern at whatever point you find yourself and shift over to the new and take up where you left off or wherever you can come back into your new pathway. Exit the old and re-enter the new and proceed from there. Do not waste time being distracted with guilt, shame, and self-punishment.

> **Leaving the old behind will be a fight, but you will win!**

After you come out of those emotional distractions, which are also old destructive patterns themselves, you still have to focus on the new and proceed in the new pathway. Every few hours that you practice the new pathway, it will get stronger and more developed. Eventually, it will turn into a pattern that gets easier and stronger and more comfortable. As this happens, the old pattern will become less and less powerful in you.

This is encouraging news that should give you hope to continue on the new pathway! When the old comfort zones and promptings call out to you to come back, just say "NO!" and let the old messages pass on by.

You don't have to be afraid of them or be concerned because they are still speaking to you. They are still activating because you taught them to do so and you trained them to be there. Maybe you didn't realize you were doing this, but the old patterns are developed by believing in them and practicing them. So for a while, the neurons (energy) will still fire on the old behaviors, but soon the old ones will subside. The longer you embrace and experience positive results with the new way of believing and functioning, the harder it will ever be to return to the old destructive patterns.

As I have taught in previous chapters, there will be a six-month time period from the time you begin a change until the time that new behavior becomes automatic. During that time, there will be an internal struggle and battle because your system is reprogramming and new pathways, emotions, and muscle memory are being formed and encoded. While this new programming is being developed, the old programs will also still be working to some extent. Those old programs will still produce thoughts, impulses, emotions, sensations, memories, and promptings related to the old behavior patterns.

During this time you may have two sets of emotions, internal messages, and promptings to act on old and new behaviors at the same time. Do not be afraid of it. The struggle is normal. Push through it and stay focused and renewed on the new thinking and behavior.

After 30 days, three months, and then six months, the old programmed patterns will get less powerful and not as automatic. Your new patterns will develop and become easier, more automatic, and therefore more natural. As the new gets stronger, the old will get weaker and weaker.

You are winning, and you are going to win!

Chapter 13

Steps Required for Lasting Change

There are specific and necessary steps that will produce productive change. In order to permanently change, you must resolve the past, identify and remove old destructive patterns, replace them with new productive ones, and practice the new ones until the new patterns become automatic. Removing or refraining from the old patterns without productive replacement is not permanent change. There must be an actual replacement of the old.

You can stop self-medicating with alcohol and replace it with another addiction, but that's not a productive replacement. Instead, you can stop self-medicating with alcohol abuse and replace it by healing the wounds and then by using your gifts and talents. This will produce deep fulfillment and productive, long-lasting change.

If an unwanted, negative or destructive behavior is stopped but not replaced with a new, productive one, then you will always default back to your old destructive patterns or you will replace the bad behavior with another unwanted, negative, or destructive pattern. This is a law of behavior.

The law is on your side

The law of behavior will never change, and it is not a respecter of persons. It is a law from which nobody will ever escape. It will always work the same way every day. It will either hurt you or benefit you.

Remember, using your personal gifts will always bring fulfillment and not using them will always produce a void and lack of fulfillment. Your gifts should be utilized to impact other people spiritually and eternally in some way so that those gifts will have eternal purpose. When the real you, a created spirit being, leaves the physical body you occupy right now, the only thing that will matter will be if and how you fulfilled your eternal purpose and used your God-given gifts and personality strengths.

But remember, permanent change always includes changes in your thinking, and the law of behavior is on your side.

> If time healed or improved things, then everyone over 40 years of age would have no issues ... and that's not the case at all!

STEPS TOWARD CHANGE

Change requires certain steps, which I describe in the following way:

Step #1 — Admit

Confess the destructive behaviors as a pattern and the way they are acted out and related to your personal behavior rather than seeing the destructive behaviors as a periodic exception to your most frequent behaviors. Do not minimize them or they will stay alive and negatively affect your thinking, decisions, responses, emotions, attitude, and behaviors.

Step #2 — Forgive

Forgive others, self, and God, and ask forgiveness from God and others. Forgiveness first releases you from the "debt" and the burden of carrying the debt that is owed you by others who have hurt and offended you. That burden requires too much energy and management of your internal resources and will eventually depress you. Let it go with your confessions so that you are emotionally, spiritually, and mentally free.

Remember, forgiveness does not condone the wrongful or sinful acts of others, but it does free you from the torment of the past hurts and the emotional and mental prison bars that unforgiveness creates.

Step #3 — Identify

Identify additional destructive behaviors as patterns by labeling your top 10 personal "faults" (example: overeating, rage, fleeing, mood swings, adultery, pornography, withdrawing, controlling, not affectionate, etc.).

Step #4 — Say "No!"

Close the door of your will and adopt a "zero-tolerance" to destructive behavior. No longer be willing to permit the behavior under any circumstance and denounce all supporting justifications.

Step #5 — Invalidate

No longer believe, obey, justify, be afraid of, legitimize, yield to, serve, embrace, or practice the old programs. An old program is a learned behavior that involves thoughts, emotions, responses, and actions (including spoken words). The behavior becomes a "program" when it is practiced for a minimum six months, at which time that behavior will become automatic.

Invalidate it by no longer believing, bonding with, obeying, protecting, justifying, or wanting that behavior and its consequences. *Webster's New American Dictionary* defines the meaning of the word "invalidate" this way; "to weaken or to make valueless." This means that you must stop placing value on your old behaviors and any related thinking that promotes them. In doing so, you will begin to dismantle your old programs.

This should involve denouncing the old behaviors and you should use the exact words. It is my experience as a therapist that making that kind of absolute and aggressive confession puts a separation between you and your old program. It helps you cut it off when you hear yourself say that you denounce it!

When you are breaking old programs that have been inside of you and ruled you, you cannot be passive in removing them. You must be aggressive and consistent. You must have a "fire burning" in your soul to absolutely remove them from your life and no longer tolerate them being inside of you.

Denouncing also dismantles the supporting beliefs regarding their validity and importance to you on a personal level. When the old programs are no longer personal to you and no longer a part of your identity, then you will no longer embrace, obey, practice, be afraid of, bond with, or validate them as truth. *Webster's* defines denounce as, "to announce formally the termination of." When you denounce the old programmed behaviors from your life, you are announcing that they no longer have the permission or the right to be valued by you. They no longer have validity!

What you do not water will not grow.

This means they are now your enemy ... the enemy of your health and of your very purpose in life. Your life's purpose and meaning no longer includes the old ways of thinking and doing. You are now determined to be different and attain different results that are fulfilling and good.

From a clinical perspective, as you no longer validate the old programs, then the corresponding neurological transmitters will stop "firing" on those programs and their behaviors and eventually the behavioral pathways will shut down. These pathways are actually activity dependent and fed by the neurotransmitters. If neurotransmitters no longer "fire" on the old behavior, then that behavioral pathway will cease to flow through the central nervous system and the body. Understanding this process reinforces why productive change never is really "accidental" at all! It is a pre-designed process.

Permanent change is hard, but it produces freedom, health, and wholeness. I often say that if you are going to suffer whether you change or not, then you might as well suffer and experience a good result rather than suffering and experiencing a bad result. Remember this profound truth: If you do the work, it will always work, for if you do the work and plant the seed, you cannot stop the results.

Step #6 — Pre-Program

Decide in advance to recognize and act (you cannot wait until the old pattern is deactivated to decide on a new course of action) on your new plans to change. Pre-programming includes these two parts:

> 1) **Prevention:** recognize the triggers, patterns, feelings, and nature in advance and do not engage. Let it pass by internally and externally.
>
> 2) **Intervention:** Stop practicing the old thoughts and behaviors and fears as soon as you recognize the old patterns at work and give yourself time to ramp down the emotions and come out of it.
> Do not be discouraged if the old program still functions for a while after you start the change process. It is normal during the transition time of removing and replacing old patterns with new ones for both the new program and old one to operate at the same time. Eventually, the old patterns will become less constant and powerful and the new ones will become more powerful and automatic. You must force yourself to practice the new patterns until they become the new automatic program, and they will. Just continue to intervene into the old ones and practice the new ones as often as you can, and the positive change will happen for you.

Step #7 — Replacement

Any time you remove an old behavior you have to replace it with a new one. Replacement must not be left to chance, emotional impulse, or moods. It must be planned and orchestrated in advance of the new behavior being acted out. Remember, just because you plan a good behavior does not mean that you are a fake, hypocrite, or not real. Some people believe that if their behavior is not impulsive or emotionally motivated that it is not real or authentic. This type of thinking is destructive and incorrect. It's a false belief.

Instead, design a model of behavior in advance, pray over it, and then begin to practice just what you have planned. You can be just as authentic and sincere with pre-planned productive behavior as you thought you were with the impulsive, motivated behavior, and even more so because it is well thought out and based upon good thinking instead of on negative or wounded thinking.

Freedom is to be the norm!

If you desire to stay free, not just get free, then you must embrace and practice your new patterns with aggression, determination, and desperation until that new productive pattern integrates into your mind and central nervous system as "normal." Remember, whatever is practiced the most encodes as normal and a comfort in that behavior will develop.

Once the freedom process has begun inside of your spirit, emotions, mind, and body, that freedom will also be normal on a cellular level. It also means that the information stored in the new programs has replaced the corresponding emotions, impulses, internal messages, emotional memory, mental memory, muscle memory, and themes. You have replaced the old patterns!

THE LAW OF SOWING AND REAPING EXPLAINED

We have already discussed this law briefly, but I want to describe it in further detail. Galatians 6:6-9 says, "Whatsoever a man sows (plants seed), that and that only is what he will reap (results)." Many parents and authority figures will use this verse to say how bad behavior will reap bad consequences, but I assure you this law of the universe works on the productive side of results as well.

The Law of Sowing and Reaping involves planting a seed into soil that produces corresponding fruit that is then harvested. Before the seed can be planted, the soil must be prepared, and before this there must be vision for the harvest or desired result. More specifically, this law must be described in detail and understood so that your potential can be maximized.

I will explain this law in the following steps and explanations:

Step #1 — Vision

Envision the desired harvest (vision for the future and desired results and how they will be used). This will determine the necessary soil, seed, water, and resources that will keep you from mediocrity, fear, minimizing potential, or busywork.

Step #2 — Cultivate the ground

Soften the ground and remove distractions (rocks and hard places), prepare, and plan.

Step #3 — Plant seed into the soil

The seed is information that goes into your mind (the soil) and your mind will automatically process it. The mind does not argue over the quality of the seed, future results, or whether it's the right seed or fruit. The mind simply accepts it.

Step #4 — Water and fertilize the seed

Practice and feed the seed by encouraging it through prayer, scripture, confessions, etc.

Step #5 — Protect the seed and fruit

Guard your garden from predators, damage, or theft. This enables your fruit to grow without interruption. Also guard and examine yourself so that you don't make decisions that could harm or hinder your harvest. Stay on course and be patient, as Galatians

6:9 says, "Do not grow weary in well doing for in due season you shall reap if you faint not" (KJV).

Step #6 — Harvest

Remain in position to benefit from your fruit (results). Collect your fruit and apply it. Do not waste the fruit of your labor.

FRUIT IS WHAT YOU WANT

Remember, reprogramming and producing desired results takes place in both your mind and your central nervous system. This is how learned behavior is developed and governed. Learned behavior is broken down into two essential parts or behavioral laws (the Law of the Mind and the Law of Action).

As I have stated, these laws of behavior are laws that work like gravity and they work the same way every time and will not change for anyone, no matter how much we try to change the law and be the exception to the rule.

In parallel, the laws of behavior work for or against everyone. The end result is the fruit of your labor, and fruit is measurable and cannot lie. The Bible (Matthew) says that you will fully know them ... and recognize them by their fruit. The two words "know" and "recognize" show that whether far away or close up, the fruit of a person's life is visible.

Fruit is how you really measure the progress of your own life. Because fruit speaks louder than words, fruit is an actual measurement of your intentions and desires. Your fruit shows if you are not willing to do everything it takes to get those results and it shows if you are making progress despite the negative comments of those around you.

Fruit is how you measure the progress of your own life.

Some say they are really "sincere" about making a change, but fruit (results) is the only accurate measuring tool for sincerity. They can talk all day or for years about dreams and visions, but fruit they can eat and enjoy will never come until they are really willing to do what it takes to produce the fruit.

It is fruit that you want. If you aren't getting the fruit you want, then change your beliefs, thoughts, habits, and patterns. Keep going and growing until you see the correct, positive sprouts come out of the ground, then cultivate them until they bring you the fruit you want. Throw out the old beliefs if they aren't bringing you life.

Keep growing, for your fruit will come!

CHAPTER 14

TARGET YOUR THOUGHTS TO TAKE CONTROL

New thoughts produce new emotions. If you want to change an undesired emotion, then the thoughts that create and induce those emotions must be targeted and changed. But if you target the emotion without changing the thoughts, then that emotion will merely be suppressed and not be actually changed.

This is why "anger management" techniques are often not permanently successful. Anger management usually focuses on managing, coping, or controlling the anger rather than dismantling the cause of the uncontrolled, compulsive anger or rage itself.

The undesirable negative emotion you are feeling should be traced back in order to identify the thoughts that generate that emotion, and then that specific thought should be targeted and changed. When the thought is changed and replaced with a new productive one, then the negative emotion will change from the old negative one to a new positive one.

HOW TO CHANGE YOUR EMOTIONS

Emotions are created by thoughts, so when you change your thoughts, your corresponding emotions will change as well. That is why your thought patterns are so important, for they will determine your beliefs, emotions, and behaviors.

If you want to change a certain area of your life, then you should spend most of your time focusing on the way you think in that specific area of your life. Investigate your own thinking. Why do you think the way you do? Do not just justify your thinking because it belongs to you!

The profound point is this: You can change your own thinking. You have the power to do it!

If you will create and practice new thoughts, they will download from the conscious to the subconscious and unconscious mind. When you practice the behavior related to that new thinking, it will turn into patterns of behavior that your central nervous system will see as normal. As I have taught in previous chapters, neurological transmitters will fire in the direction of your most frequently acted on behavior on any given topic and develop neurological pathways. This process is a law of our system. It will work for you every time, without fail.

As you practice new thoughts, then they will eventually produce new normal emotions. If those thoughts and emotions are positive, then you will experience normal and automatic positive thoughts.

New thoughts will eventually produce new normal emotions.

Again, this does not happen accidentally and without practice. You have to be serious about feeling differently and do what it takes to feel differently. You may be very serious, desperate, and hurting, but if you are not willing to do what it takes, then all the hurting in the world will not make you change or transform. Being miserable is not a strong enough motivator. You must choose to change, and then follow through with that choice. Make yourself practice your new thinking, regardless of how hard it is. Just keep practicing and it will work for you.

I read that Henry Ford, Alexander Bell, and Harry Firestone built houses next to each other. I believe this was so that they could influence each other in a positive and innovative way. I do not believe it was for the purpose of excluding other people. In a similar way, you will have to choose "neighbors." Will it be people who are more successful and more knowledgeable than you in certain areas of life or will it be people you feel comfortable with but who lack the fruit that you want?

If you ask for help, most people will be willing to help you. Even if you are afraid of rejection, do not listen to the fear. Reach and ask for help and express a desire to know more than you know. There is no shame in asking, but there is shame in not asking for help.

Ditch the destructive patterns

Destructive patterns are recurring behaviors that are consistent in nature and logic, but are not behaviors that you want in your life. These destructive behaviors, typically developed from wounds or learned from parents or caretakers, have downloaded into your mind and central nervous system as automatic programs, with "files" attached, and are seen as "normal" behavior. These are activated (triggered) by a topic that reminds your brain of a past negative experience or wound. (These triggering mechanisms are also called brain associations. A brain association is simply when you think about a person, place, or thing in the present tense and they remind you of something else you experienced in the past, be it good or bad.)

You must replace the old, destructive patterns with new, positive ones. It can only become permanent after you remove and replace the old pattern. Removing or stopping is not sufficient, for the old pattern must be dismantled and completely replaced. Think long-term change. Short-term change suppresses things, but the trigger is still there.

The crisis or trauma often brings about short-term change, for when the crisis ends, the behavior defaults back to the old pattern. For example, a husband stops/reduces getting drunk or looking at porn when his wife leaves/threatens to leave, but he resumes when she comes back to him.

Here are six steps to ditching, permanently, the destructive patterns that you do not want in your life:

Step #1 — *Identify your new desired behaviors*

What do you want? Choose the behaviors that will produce the designed and improved results that you want. Don't look for a temporary change.

Step #2 — *Convert the old to the new*

Choose what you want, and then go after it. Replace the old with the new. Will you listen or lash out? Control or train? Lie or tell the truth? Be faithful or unfaithful? Be pure or impure? Pray or not? Attend church or not? Forgive or not? Love or hate?

Replace the old with the new.

Step #3 — *Transition from old to new*

When you are in the process of change, the old program files and new ones being developed (thoughts, emotions, beliefs, behavior) will both function periodically at the same time. This is totally normal, so don't let it cause fear, worry, doubt, or confusion. The change is indeed taking place. Relax. It takes time and practice to invalidate and dismantle the old programs and establish the new programs as normal in your mind and central nervous system,

The same law of the mind and law of action (laws of behavior) that established the old patterns are now being used to establish the new ones. As we've discussed, the new behaviors will become patterns when habits are formed, which occurs after about 30 days of practice (not just 30 days of time passing) and after about six months of practicing the new productive behaviors.

Change is taking place!

The exception to this behavioral rule is when addictions are being removed and replaced. With addictions, it takes approximately six months for a new habit to be formed and about 1-3 years for automatic behavior (character) to be formed. However, the process of change can begin after only 10 minutes of practice!

This transition also involves seeing yourself differently. When you see yourself change your thinking and behavior and walk it out over time, then your self-image will conform to the new way of doing things. Eventually your self-image becomes your identity. This is when you actually identify yourself as the new person, the new you. Of course becoming this new person does not mean you lose your core personality. Rather, it means that you lose your old learned behavior personality and find your core once again.

A transition takes place when you create a passage from one state, place, or stage to another. You can actually watch the shift occurring inside yourself. Then you experience a separation from the old life and bond more with the new way. The new way gradually becomes more automatic and more comfortable in you and becomes the new norm.

This transition occurs on the inside of you first, and then it shows on the outside. If the change is outward only, then it is short-term and you will default back to the old behaviors.

Step #4 — Establish new patterns

You know what to do.

Step #5 — Develop a new habit

You have your new patterns.

Step #6 — Develop a new character

Your new character becomes your new automatic behavior.

A REAL EXAMPLE

A married couple came to my office and at first they said they were there because of the wife's rages and fits. She would pull the tablecloth off the table, throwing everything to the floor. She would yell and scream.

Upon further research, beyond their initial presentation, I found that she had been sexually abused by her uncle as an adolescent ... but that was not all.

Regarding her uncle, she told her mom and dad, but they had not believed her. They said, "If it did happen, then you must have done something to induce him." They claimed her charge was false and simply to get attention.

Many years later, she married a man who would invalidate and abuse her as well. If she didn't do all he wanted, he would shove her (in bra and panties) out the front door so neighbors could see her and he would lock the door. Eventually, back in the house, she would go into a rage. It was a culmination of past and present hurts. She was hurt, and in her rage she would do things. Her wound was deep, and from the depths, the rage came out.

You have to go to the root of the problem. You have to dig to the bottom, not just look at the image of the problem.

It is interesting that people marry similar personality types, which is really a form of trauma bonding. They don't know it, but it continues the trauma, and it's a similar trauma.

After finding the core truth, the molestation by her uncle, I tried to have her go back to her parents, to heal that relationship (many times the parents aren't dead), but in this case the parents were dead, she couldn't go back and be validated.

Then we worked on her abuse, and if she wasn't too scared, to forgive and say the words to her abuser. (Through this, the victim forgives, and that releases the pain of the wound and emotions of the wound. It opens the door and brings a release of all the emotions that are trapped inside.) She confessed it and prayed and let it go. She said the words she always wanted to say. (I coach people through it. I want them to purge it out. I want them to cry it out. I want them to release it and get it out of them. Afterward, they do have relief from it. I ask probing, hard questions, and after they release it, they walk out free. It's a "finally" thing. There is a core spiritual and emotional healing that comes with a sincere confession and letting go of hurts, traumas, wounds, and offenses.) For her, it was a time of healing.

From 20 years of this therapy, I found this:

- Confession to God = forgiveness and cleansing
- Confession to man = healing and restoration

1 John 1:9 says, "If we confess our sins, He is faithful and just and will forgive us our sins and purify us from all unrighteousness" (NIV).

James 5:16 says, "Confess to one another therefore your faults (your slips, your false steps, your offenses, your sins) and pray [also] for one another, that you may be healed and restored [to a spiritual tone of mind and heart]. The earnest (heartfelt, continued) prayer of a righteous man makes tremendous power available [dynamic in its working]. Confess your faults one to another so you can be healed and restored to a spiritual…" (AMP).

This is a very functional and true principle.

You must identify the wound you are confessing so that the wound you are confessing lets out the emotions from the wound. You tap into the wound, know what it's called, know the emotions, and then the emotions come out with the words. This comes out with crying, moaning, sighs, tears, bawling, or nothing. After that, there is relief and freedom. Different personalities manifest this differently.

SET YOUR NEW BELIEFS

Beliefs are the information you receive and establish as truth. In order to produce long-term change, you must realize that thoughts produce beliefs and those beliefs go on to produce and support behavior. In order to change a belief, you must identify and label correctly what you believe and why you believe it.

You will find that destructive or negative beliefs, which support destructive or negative behaviors, were probably established by a negative or traumatic experience. These destructive beliefs are a type of wound behavior, so you must heal the wound and reprogram your old beliefs. You cannot continue to validate the old beliefs just because you are familiar with them or because of pride or fear. An unwanted belief must be identified on any given topic and removed by deciding that it is invalid and no longer received as truth.

For example, a belief that your father did not love you because he did not spend time with you can be removed when you learn that he was sick for many years. That new information is received as truth and your old belief of not being loved is no longer validated.

Subsequently, all of the corresponding thoughts, behaviors, and emotions that were associated and empowered by the old belief are no longer valid or practiced.

> You can choose the positive beliefs you want.

Mark 9:23 says, "Everything is possible for him who believes" (NIV). This verse is true from every aspect and level, whether people have destructive and unhealthy beliefs, or healthy and productive beliefs. Even if people believe something that minimizes their potential in life and produces negative consequences, all destructive things are possible within that destructive belief system. On the contrary, all things are also possible within a productive belief system. Either way, all things are possible.

If your life is full of bad consequences, it is because of your decisions, and behind your decisions are your beliefs. The only way to stop the bad consequences is to evaluate what you believe about that destructive behavior and accept the possibility that you have beliefs that are unhealthy. Then you must lower your pride and stubbornness and humble yourself so that you can let go of that old belief and insert a new, good one. In a way, you can use your selfishness to improve yourself instead of destroying yourself.

Any belief can be invalidated and altered. Just trace the bad behavior back to the belief that supports that behavior and the bad choices. Denounce it so that you can create space between you and the old belief. Then invalidate it by believing that the old belief is no longer your ally and no longer good for you. Then stop practicing it immediately. Decide what belief you will put in its place and receive the new belief as the truth. Then immediately practice the new beliefs and corresponding behaviors that go with it until they become normal.

Do not stop because it gets difficult. Do not think in terms of whether this is hard or easy! It can be hard at first, but the good leads to life and the bad leads to death. You must choose life in everything you do.

Beliefs come in two forms:

1) Independent beliefs

These beliefs are stand-alone beliefs that are not dependent on another belief to be truth or valid for you. For example: God is real, water hydrates my body, I am married, my spouse was unfaithful to me, my parents abused me, fear is real, controlling helps me feel safe, etc.

These independent beliefs may or may not be true, but they stand alone.

2) Dependent beliefs

These beliefs exist and are true (in you) because the corresponding Independent beliefs are true. For example: because God is real I have hope, because water hydrates it benefits my body when I drink it, because I am married I can trust him/her, because my spouse was unfaithful I cannot trust again, because my parents abused me I must not be valuable or worthy, because fear is real it is telling me the truth about the impending danger messages I feel, because control makes me feel safe then if I do not control I am not safe, etc.

Specific beliefs, or series of beliefs, regarding any subject make up your belief system. This belief system is a network of beliefs that are connected together to promote and support the subject to which they are attached. With that said, you typically act out what you believe.

RENEWING YOUR MIND

Renewing your mind involves removing old, nonproductive beliefs and replacing them with new ones, by design.

However, you cannot complete the renewing process of your mind by simply inserting new truths into your thinking. At the core level, renewing involves removing old beliefs, pre-designing new ones, then inserting them into your mind and heart in place of the old ones. You must remove and then replace.

After you have removed the old beliefs and replaced them with new ones, then you must follow it up with reinforcing the beliefs over and over until that new way of thinking becomes normal and becomes a part of your belief system.

You want to strip yourself of those old beliefs, to develop a "zero tolerance" for them, and to "brain wash" yourself with your new productive beliefs. (I don't mind using that phrase because the old unhealthy beliefs also brainwashed you.)

Inserting new truths is not enough.

People often protect and continue in unhealthy beliefs because those bad beliefs belong to them and they are subconsciously trying to validate themselves. In protecting bad beliefs they are really trying to bring validation to themselves. This is why people fight to keep old unhealthy beliefs. Another reason is that their old beliefs are familiar and their identity is wrapped up in the old beliefs, even though the beliefs are unhealthy. People who lack purpose feel inferior and are insecure. As a result, they try to hold on to beliefs, things, relationships, and behaviors so they can maintain some feeling of control of their otherwise unstable lives. Don't ever do that. Instead:

Step #1: Remove!

Remove the old beliefs that promote old behaviors by identifying them, not validating, not practicing, and not obeying them. Denounce them verbally.

Step #2: Replace!

Replace and enforce the new beliefs you want. Remind yourself through thoughts, confessions, prayer, notes, friends, counseling, and teachings of your new beliefs and the related behaviors you are practicing. It will help you replace the old with the new.

Personality Types and Personality Languages

You are no doubt familiar with the four basic personality types. Well, each personality type has a personality language associated with it, which simply means that you need to speak to a person with his/her personality strengths and weaknesses in mind rather than trying to relate to them with your personality traits and preferences. This only makes commonsense.

Many people use the term "love language," but I like to use the term "personality language" because a love language comes from personality characteristics and preferences.

I will briefly explain the different personality types and their strengths and weaknesses:

Personality #1: outgoing, task oriented, non people-person

Strengths include: being direct, decisive, result-oriented, establishes goals, self-manager, to the point, no social fears, and says it like it is, persistent, determined, fast thinker.

Weaknesses are: being harsh, uses people to get their desired results, angry or agitated if inconvenienced, no empathy, overlooks details if not necessary for immediate results, impatient, dominating, does not support other people's success if it threatens their results, can sacrifice relationship closeness if it interferes with their intended results, selfish by thinking of the results they want, stubborn.

Personality #2: outgoing, people-person

Strengths include: being friendly, risk-taker, passionate, likes variety, attention-getter, influences people, optimistic, talkative, enthusiastic, fast thinker, image oriented (how they are perceived/viewed by others is important, uses imagination, feeds off of the environment/mood), spontaneous, good with people and in front of crowds, they usually look good, influencer, does better with recognition.

Weaknesses are: having a lot of acquaintances but few real friends, optimistic and overlooks details that can and will hurt them, gets bored too easily…has to stay active and busy, sacrifices fruitful work for fun and stimulation, impulsive (emotionally escalates), gets offended quickly, superficial, focus on improving their image more than their internal maturity…image matters too much, lashes out if made to look bad (real or perceived), they lie or change their words so they will not look bad.

Personality #3: reserved, people-person

Strengths include: being satisfied with private/personal appreciation (not recognition), servant, helps people (get out of problems, improve, succeed), encourages people, team player, fulfilled by getting results for other people, empathetic, people pleaser, self-sacrificing, nice, soft spoken, and having close emotional connections.

Weaknesses are: codependent (emotionally, self-image, self-worth), feels guilty when hasn't done anything wrong, pleases the users and gets used, takes on false responsibilities and feels guilty if they do not, stays deeply hurt for a long time when not appreciated, gets personally involved in a relationship out of feeling sorry for someone then can't end the relationship because they do not want to hurt their feelings.

Personality #4: reserved, task oriented, non people-person

Strengths include: being analytical, detailed oriented, advanced planner, creates controlled environment, good listener, accuracy is important, black and white precise standards, predictable, consistent, thinks before speaking.

Weaknesses are: obsesses in their thoughts (rehearses the same thoughts over and over trying not to miss a detail but with no new answers), controlling, resistant to change (even if the change is good for them), "passive aggressive" (feel just as many emotions as someone expressive but suppresses them and stuffs them down on the inside), assumes they have communicated but did not use their actual words, have many more thoughts than they use words and remember speaking words they only thought in their mind, accuse others of their own negative thoughts or behaviors, create thought-induced fears and anxieties or worries.

If you can understand both strengths and weaknesses, you can play to your strengths while minimizing your weaknesses. Furthermore, you do not expect others to be strong in areas where they are weak.

Chapter 15

Put Emotions in Their Place

Being motivated to act in some way because of your feelings and emotions is what I call "feeling motivated." Many people feel motivated in a crisis, their senses are aware of danger, but when the crisis subsides or is over, they go back to their old thinking and behaviors.

What's more, feelings are not an accurate way to determine if a crisis is over. This is because you can feel okay and still might not have solved the problem or you can feel uncomfortable and the problem might be solved.

Feelings and emotions can change, depending on your particular sensitivities and emotional make up. Just because you feel better does not mean you have permanently changed or that you are permanently healthy. Emotions do not provide a true assessment of you situation.

Emotions do, however, give you an idea of how stable you are. But emotions do not equip you to be stable and solve problems. Yes, you will have emotions, but they are not a steady guide for helping you think through a problem. In fact, in order to think through problems, you must be trained to make quality decisions while you are feeling your emotions.

There's no rush

Outside of true imminent danger, most problems do not have to be solved right on the spot. The best responses are usually ones that are thought out and are not reactionary or impulsive. Problems that are emotionally motivated are impulsive or compulsive. These kinds of reactions to any given situation will have to be corrected after you work through your emotions. It is wisdom to not make decisions, especially long-lasting ones, while you are emotionally ramped up or unstable.

To be unstable emotionally doesn't necessarily mean that you are mentally ill. Rather, it means that your emotions are creating instability for you and you have to learn how to work through that emotional state and make decisions after you calm down. Another good way to respond to your emotional distress is to establish some baseline ways of thinking that are life principles, and refer to them instead of referring to your emotions when you need to know what to do in any situation.

There are some instances when your emotions will distract you even if you have pre-planned ways of thinking programmed into your mind. In these cases your mind will clear within a few minutes and allow you to decide what you need to do. If you need help, of course call for help. I always say that there is no shame in asking for help.

THINK RATHER THAN REACT

People usually take some time recovering emotionally from a crisis or even an average problem. It is important that you develop a healthy way to think and function in any given situation. You must train and equip yourself to know how to think rather than react out of emotion.

With God involved in your development, you will be empowered by Him to help in your thinking so that you will rule your emotions and your emotions will not rule you. You don't have to improve yourself alone and in your own strength. Ask God to help you and He will. You are not always strong enough to face every problem and situation in your own strength. The fact is that your own strength will never be totally adequate. You will always need God to empower you.

Maybe with the small things in life you believe that you can do well without Him and have a sense of empowerment without God.

As a therapist who deals with every human problem, I can tell you that there will come a time in your life when you will need Him desperately. Without Him, you will not have the strength to make it through. Ask Him to help you now, rather than having to later on.

> **Being comfortable may not be a sign of being healthy.**

In healthy decision making rather than fear-based control, you must use knowledge, wisdom, understanding, discretion, and discernment to guide and protect you — not your emotions. Again, emotions are not an accurate measuring tool for personal health.

Imagine having a growth on your body. Is it cancerous? Then you find out that it's simply a harmless fatty tumor. Until you learned the truth, wouldn't you experience panic and an array of negative and unstable emotions? That is exactly why I often say that emotions do not tell the truth.

I have counseled clients who felt comfortable in their sexual, porn, or substance addictions, but they were nonetheless in bondage and ruled by their problems. Eventually their addictions ruined their marriages and relationships with their children and sometimes their professional careers. They were comfortable with their denial, yet their emotions did not tell them the truth about the upcoming consequences of their addictions.

The feelings are real, but they do not usually tell the truth. I have also counseled clients and have observed others who were emotionally uncomfortable with prayer. Certainly in this case their emotions of discomfort were not telling them the truth. They were uncomfortable with God, probably because they were unfamiliar with prayer or with His presence. Or maybe they were uncomfortable with God because of their secret sins they try so hard to conceal. God is love and is the author of life, not death. He is actually the one to turn to when you have these types of problems, rather than run from Him. He is aware of what is happening on the inside of you and He is the very one who is helping you through it and giving you another chance to live! You do not have to be good, perfect, or get yourself "straightened out" before you pray to Him. You can come just as you are. Confess your sins and He is faithful and just to forgive and cleanse you.

Sin is something that has violated you and that creates separation between you and God. If you need to, seek out someone who can help you spiritually and can pray with you. It is not a sign of weakness to pray, but a sign of strength and wisdom. It is okay if you are not powerful enough by yourself because no one is in every circumstance.

Don't ask your feelings for permission

Feeling motivation also means that you are using feelings to determine whether or not you can or will take action in any regard. In this case, the emotion is actually controlling your decisions, which means that you believe your emotions are telling you the truth. This type of conditioning makes you inconsistent and unpredictable. It makes you a slave to your own emotions.

Again, emotions and feelings are real and are often very powerful, but they are not necessarily telling you the truth. There is a difference between real and true. Your emotions send you internal messages and sensations throughout your body. This is because emotions possess energy in them. This is why they are powerful.

> **Emotions and feelings are real, but that doesn't make them true.**

Then emotions are usually followed by secondary feelings that were created by your response to having the emotions and feelings. This is similar to a panic attack or disorder. The panic is caused by a set of fear-oriented thoughts or beliefs. Then the uncomfortable feeling that panic brings with it creates a whole new fear of having another attack. This fear is in addition to the fear that originally caused the panic attack.

Please note that when a fear is developed from a true traumatic experience, the fear feels more legitimate when it says that there is impending danger again. The fear becomes more believable when it was birthed from an actual tangible trauma rather than being formed from mere imagination.

Both are imagined, but trauma-based fear can be very tormenting. Scripture says that fear has torment and that is very true. I have found that fear-based feelings are the most powerful negative feelings that you can experience.

- Fear motivates people to sabotage good relationships for fear that they will experience betrayal just like their parents did.
- Fear will motivate you to abandon the relationship before they can hurt you.
- Fear says that if you create failure, then somehow it is really not failure because you caused it, which makes it different than really going all out and then not being good enough to succeed.
- Fear can motivate you to settle for a relationship that you know is bad for you simply because you are afraid that you won't get anyone any better or you are afraid of being lonely or afraid of hurting their feelings.

I am not suggesting that you should be mean and not consider the welfare of another person. I am instead suggesting that you make relationship decisions out of wise compatibility measurements rather than out of fear. When you wake up from fear motivation, you will come to a very rude awakening that fear has lied to you and did not motivate you to make the best decisions for you.

SOME THINGS NEVER CHANGE

If your emotions and feelings are founded in some type of fear, then you need to know that the fear message never changes and therefore the emotions will always feel the same. Fear will always send messages (mental or physical) that there is some potential or impending danger that is known or unknown (fear of the unknown).

Fear also makes you think and feel that you are inadequate to protect yourself from the fear and from being victimized by it. Again, the danger may not even be true danger, but the feelings and internal messages produced by the fear are real — you really do feel them. You must not believe these emotions just because they are real.

Why? Fear emotions do not tell you the truth. As I have said, fear-oriented emotions are the most powerful negative motivators of any feelings and emotions. They are the ones most people struggle with on all levels, regardless of their personality type.

On a technical note, even though emotions and feelings are very similar, the key difference between them is that emotions are generated from thoughts only, while feelings are connected to experience, physical contact, or touch. But for the purposes of explaining feeling motivation, I often commingle the two phrases without making distinction between the two.

LOVE IS THE STRONGEST

Love feelings and emotions are the strongest positive motivators in the universe. Scripture says that love never fails and that is the truth. Love overcomes fear and sometimes even overcomes logic. Love makes people think that everything will turn out all right.

Along with love, I also encourage you to use wisdom. Love and wisdom will guide you correctly and protect you. As you know, fear will not protect you. (You can be afraid and still act with wisdom.) You will experience fear throughout your lifetime, but fear is not your productive motivator. My advice is to be motivated by love, which overcomes fear and wisdom, for it will protect and guide you.

> **Love and wisdom will guide you where you want to go.**

I believe it is imperative that you get to a place where you are no longer willing to obey, believe, trust, embrace, or validate feelings as your motivators in life. If you are ruled by your emotions, you are placing emotions out of their productive order, which places them outside of their created purpose.

Feeling motivation will convince you to unconditionally validate your emotions and do as they tell you. They will also require that you make other people validate your emotions, and if they do not, it feels like they are personally rejecting you. The more you practice this type of emotional pattern, the more normal it will become. You will also develop a false belief that those extreme emotions are just an expression of the core you and if people would just accept your emotions (even if it includes irrational behavior) then they would be accepting you personally. Nothing could be further from the truth! The fact is that those emotions are not a reflection of the real you. God did not create and design you to be ruled by emotions and feelings. He designed you to be led by wisdom and love.

QUESTION YOURSELF

Emotions can be preprogrammed by practicing them or they can be triggered by thoughts, memories, words, and associations. Either way, if you believe that emotions are good motivators and are a measurement of true reality, then you will obey them.

But you can break this pattern by beginning to question emotions and their validity. Run all of your emotions through the filter of wisdom. Wisdom will ask you, "Is this decision you are making going to give you the result that brings life to you?"

Think in terms of life and death. Always make decisions that produce life (spiritual, mental, relational, physical, academic, emotional, economical life) instead of death.

You start the change by invalidating the feeling motivation and replacing it with wise and healthy thinking. If you know that you have not been trained to think this way, then find the right person(s) who can help you think productively. If your way of thinking and your beliefs are not producing life and maximizing your potential, then your thinking must be changed. It is that straightforward.

This type of new healthiness will not be void of emotions because God created emotions. All emotions are not bad or unhealthy. However, they must not be your god and your masters who dictate your decisions and behavior. I challenge you right now to take a look at the way you act when your emotions get stronger. If you know you have emotions that rule you and tell you how to think and what to do, then you need to change that part of your life and decide to do it now. Start with admitting that you have this problem with your emotions. Maybe you feel depression or anger when you don't want to, maybe you feel intolerant of hurting people, maybe you feel anxiety when you are not in control, maybe your feelings make you misinterpret what people are saying to you, or maybe your feelings add words to your hearing to make things more personally offensive. Whatever the case may be, stop believing your emotions right now. Realize that all of your emotions are not true ... they are real but not true.

Some Christians accidentally develop a belief that their feelings "speaking" to them and God speaking to them are one and the same. This commingling of internal voices, sensations, and promptings will create confusion and make you obey your emotions and your comfort zones rather than actually hearing from God. Ask yourself what God would be saying to you if your emotions were out of the way and you had no fear, then ask God what He is inspiring or directing you to do.

THE PURPOSE FOR EMOTIONS

The purpose for emotions is to support behavior with passion, measure behavior with good or bad feelings, provide a sense of reward for good behavior and a sense of pain for bad behavior, and for pleasure and happiness. Feelings were not created to rule over your mind, behavior, and decisions. Emotions are the caboose, not the engine.

Feelings are given to us by God to experience pain to alert us to look in certain areas to see if there is a malfunction of any kind. Not to become phobic or paranoid, but to bring our attention to areas of our life and our bodies. The simplest way to say it is that God created emotions so that we can feel good when we think and act good and feel bad when we think and act bad. Feelings are positive when we think positive and negative when we think negative.

> **Emotions have a real purpose ... and it's not telling you what to do.**

Therefore, when you feel negative and bad, then you should take a look at your negative thoughts and replace them with positive ones. If the negative thoughts are a result of your unresolved and unhealed past, then open up your past and stop obeying the fear that will tell you not to open up and deal with your past. Fear will tell you to suppress it and cope with it. Coping mechanisms are necessary and helpful in some cases where there is no present solution, but why cope with it when you can resolve it.

In order to resolve the past, you must confess it and expose all of the hurts and wounds that can be either self-inflicted or inflicted by some other source. When you confess it to God and another person, this kind of exposure will immediately begin to create an inner release and healing of the painful emotions and feelings that are locked down inside of the wound.

Remember, when that emotion begins to come up from deep down inside of your gut, do not suppress or resist the release that usually manifests through crying or some type of moaning or noise from inside. Just let it happen, even if you are uncomfortable and scared. You know that fear and discomfort are not telling you the truth. There is no danger in releasing the pain. In fact, almost immediately or within a few minutes time, you will begin to feel free. An inner healing will begin to take place on the wings of your deep heartfelt confession.

God created tears, so let them flow. They are a sign of your submission and brokenness, and submission and brokenness are required to totally release and receive healing from wounds and hurts and the associated pain. During the confession of the wound, you will need to say with your mouth that you forgive anyone who has hurt you. This can include God, yourself, or others. Even though God has not abandoned you, you can feel that He has because of the hurt you have experienced. Nevertheless, forgive Him, forgive yourself, and forgive all others by name who have hurt you.

As we have discussed, saying that you forgive does not condone the wrong actions of those who have hurt you. Forgiveness first releases you from the emotional prison of unforgiveness, bitterness, resentment, offense, hate, rage, shame, and guilt. Confess it and get it forgiven and healed. Your freedom and healing must be your top priority. If you harbor the pain of your past, you are not punishing the people who hurt you ... you are punishing yourself! After you forgive and let it go, you can then use wisdom to decide what relationship, if any, to have with those people.

Fear will tell you to avoid exposure and to keep it secret. Fear will go to great lengths and make the most untruthful excuses to explain why you can't expose the truth of your wounded past and secret sins. If you keep it inside of you, it is unresolved. Confession is required. Some (not all) of those excuses sound like this:

- "It's in the past …"
- "That was a long time ago …"
- "I don't want to dig it up again …"
- "I already forgave them …"
- "They don't deserve it …"
- "I can't forgive them …"
- "I'll be hurt again …"
- "It doesn't bother me any more …"
- "God has forgiven me …"
- "Let bygones be bygones …"
- "God can't forgive …"
- "I can't forgive myself …"
- "Time heals all …"
- "It is too hard …"
- "Talking about it won't do any good …"
- "It didn't hurt me …"

To summarize, feelings are not productive or accurate motivators for making wise decisions. God did not create feelings and emotions to be your leader. He created them to be a product of your thoughts, decisions, and actions. Feelings should be a product of your productive thoughts just like they are a product of your negative and destructive thoughts.

Section VI

Steps to Maximizing Your Potential

Every person who exists or has ever existed has: potential. In your lifetime, it is very possible to reach your potential and be fulfilled by it. Noah Webster, in his 1828 *The American Dictionary of the English Language*, defined potential as, "Having power to impress on us the ideas of certain qualities, though the qualities are not inherent in the thing; as potential heat or cold"… "Anything that may be possible"… and "In possibility, not in act."

Throughout your lifetime you have had and will have opportunities to use your personality strengths, giftings, and talents to fulfill certain possibilities. In doing so, you will be fulfilled and have strength of purpose. You can make the best of every opportunity or you will minimize them or even bypass them. You have certain qualities, special endowments that never go away and will always reside on the inside of your being waiting for you to tap into them and be empowered by them. Maximize them in the greatest possible way and they will give you power to achieve.

If you do not, you will be unfulfilled in life and have a lack of purpose. By maximizing them you will be fulfilled and experience purpose in your life. You have the power to either do one or the other. Potential not used has the same outcome as not having that potential. Potential is a possibility that must be acted upon in order to unleash the power in it to fulfill you and work for you. I believe that your potential is the sum total of your God-given giftings (special endowments) and when utilized, become the fulfillment of your purpose. When you utilize them in the right venues, ways and means, you then "maximize" your potential and purpose in life. Fulfillment is within you, waiting on you.

The greatest basketball players on earth will miss 100% of the shots they don't take! The greatest athletes that ever existed only made a percentage (never 100%) of their attempts. Likewise, maximizing your potential does not mean that your efforts will be perfect. But know what you do best and do it with excellence. Train yourself to know your gifts and talents and maximize them. The simple process of maximizing your potential includes:

> Identify>label>understand>develop>utilize>maximize
> = fulfillment

Chapter 16

Maximizing Your Potential

You possess God-given potential and your greatest fulfillment in life will be experienced when you identify, label, understand, develop, utilize, and maximize your potential.

Maximized potential comes through the maximization of your personal gifts, talents, and personality strengths, all of which are the core you. The ultimate purpose and fulfillment in life comes from not just using those gifts, but from maximizing them throughout your lifetime.

How to Identify Your Gifts

The way you identify your personal gifts is to evaluate the behaviors that you act out naturally and automatically that produce personal fulfillment and passion.

Your personality strengths also align with your giftings. When you understand your personality strengths, you will have insight into your gifts because your gifts are manifested through your personality strengths (see Personality section). For example:

- People with an outgoing task personality are direct, decisive, and result-oriented. They think about results before anything else. Therefore their gifts are typically associated with some type of managing, delegating, authority, getting results, and administration.

- Those with an outgoing people-person personality like to visit, have fun, be optimistic, and think in terms of image. They are good networkers and marketers because they like to interact with people.

- People with a reserved people-person personality are servants who build relationships, help people, and need to be appreciated. Their strengths are in serving, getting results for others, and having opportunities to demonstrate their empathy in a one-on-one capacity so they can see how it pleases and helps others.

- Those with a reserved task personality are analytical, detailed, and are precise and critical thinkers. They process details and enjoy it more than they like being around people. They think and listen more than they talk, and they do well with numbers and working the task rather than interacting with people. They are also creative on a grassroots level and typically enjoy expressing themselves more through some form of artistic expression (music, drawing, painting, carpentry, computers, etc).

Our greatest weakness is the misuse of our greatest strength. Gifts and strengths are very powerful when maximized and therefore are still powerful when misused. Adolph Hitler slaughtered six million Jews, yet he was a great orator, leader, administrator, and visionary. When he misused these God-given gifts and strengths, he was very destructive. Charles Manson, a mass murderer, was a great influencer of people and knew how to develop relationships. This is how he convinced people to kill those he targeted. Gifts are powerful, even when misused.

You can never lose your gifts!

If your gift is not used and not maximized, you will experience unhappiness, lack of fulfillment, and maybe depression. Voids are created by not using your gifts.

Unfortunately these types of voids are commonly filled in a negative or destructive way. It is imperative, therefore, that you know your strengths and gifts. Use them. Maximize them. They are the true core inner you. They are your true and real identity. They are the real you.

YOUR GIFTS ARE GIFTS

A gift is a personal endowment bestowed upon you by God to fulfill a certain purpose in your lifetime. Gifts inherently reside inside of you on a core spiritual and cellular level. Gifts always fulfill you and always flow naturally out of you. When you maximize your gifts, you are fulfilling purpose.

The fact that no two people on the planet have the same fingerprint goes beyond mental comprehension as to how God could design us and provide a baseline proof that every one of us is unique.

Gifts exist to benefit the giver and the receiver of the gift, not to remain merely potential that is never used. The end result of unused potential and gifts is the same as never having that gift. Personal gifts are God-given and never go away and will always remain, regardless of time or circumstances because personal gifts are attached to and birthed from the human spirit.

Your gifts flow out of you in the form of natural and automatic propensities, exist on a cellular level, and are birthed and centered from the created human spirit. Gifts can be used for productive (God-intended) purposes or destructive purposes (as was demonstrated with Hitler), depending on the power you choose to submit to and serve.

You need to exercise your gifts. When you see talented sports figures whose abilities seem almost "supernatural" in a way, it is because they have exercised their gifts. Almost anyone can get good at something with sufficient practice, but when it's your natural gifting, that puts you two steps ahead of everyone else. No matter how hard others try, they can't seem to catch up. That's because you are operating in your gifting.

Your gifts never go away

Potential resides inside of you in the form of your gifts and personality strengths, and this potential remains in existence even if you do not believe you possess the gifts or strengths. That's because a personal gift never goes away. This is true because we are created spirit beings and gifts originate from the spirit and in the spirit level. Your spirit (the real you) never dies and will always live somewhere in eternity after your physical body dies and turns to dust. Your physical body is a "temple" of clay that is not eternal. Your spirit is eternal. Therefore your gifts are eternal because they were given to you by God before you were born and always operate on a spiritual level.

I have personally listened to the testimony of holocaust survivors. The one asset that always remained was their gift. They had everything taken from them by the Nazis, such as their clothes, family, friends, freedom, health, civil rights, and more, but when they came out they still had their personal God-given gifts. It was like riding a bicycle, you never forget, except it is even more natural than a learned behavior. It was an integral part of their being.

God created it that way for the purpose of fulfillment, prosperity, to impact society, and most importantly, to impact other people in an eternal and spiritual way during the course of your life. Everybody has the same 24 hours to maximize or minimize their time and gifts … which are you doing? What have you accomplished and who have you spiritually impacted in your lifetime? Or how many excuses have you used to live an average life?

> **Your gifts are God-given to you.**

Remove the spirit of average in yourself and begin today by making the decision to no longer tolerate in yourself an average or mediocre life. Do not start by overwhelming yourself and conquering the world. Start by lovingly helping someone and impacting that person's life, both spiritually and in a practical way. Hurting people are everywhere and they need your encouragement. When you encourage and show love to people, you will find life and fulfillment come up inside of yourself.

This is where you start. There is nothing stopping you and there is no real hindrance. Do it now and change your average self.

Fulfill your ultimate purpose in life by impacting others with God's love. In doing so you will never live another average day again.

UNDERSTANDING THE PURPOSE

Scripture says, "To everything there is a purpose" (Ecclesiastes 3:1). There is a purpose for relationships, every interaction, all friendships, tasks, objects, all behavior, etc.

Regarding the important area of relationships, you will need to create rules of engagement that align with your designed purpose. You will differentiate between close friends (where both parties productively influence equally), friends (where both parties productively influence but not equally), acquaintances (where one party influences more productively and not equally), and socializing (superficial interaction and interviewing to determine how to define the relationship and its potential purpose). It goes without saying that you want relationships to be positive and not negative.

Purpose also provides meaning for something or someone's existence. If someone operates outside of the intended productive purpose for something, that activity will immediately or eventually become negative, destructive, or inadequate to produce the desired results.

There are three types of purpose:

1. **Positional purpose:** This is typically the purpose and mission statement of an organization and expectations of the owner.

2. **Situational purpose:** This is your designed job description, which includes understanding and clarifying trust factors (sincerity, reliability, and competency), strengths, and gifts that line up with the job description.

3. **Personal purpose:** This is your private reason or motivation for the position (income, use of gifts, interaction with people, learning, developing gifts, etc.).

Understanding purpose for everything you do and every relationship you have will guard you from trauma bonding and other destructive behaviors and will also help define your goals (finish line markers that you set for yourself in order to measure your progress, including timelines for accomplishing something you plan to achieve) and boundaries (guidelines and perimeters that you should not violate or cross).

Never give up!

Since your potential is connected to your personal gifts and personality strengths (which never go away), you can always tap into them, use them, and be fulfilled. Regardless of your sins and mistakes of your past, your gifts never leave you. Again, this is because a gift is in the "DNA" of your spirit. External circumstances cannot annul or cancel your gifts.

And your God-given purpose in life is to maximize your potential. You must use the gifts God gave you in order to be fulfilled in life. If you are not fulfilled, it is because you have not yet learned to operate in your gifts.

People who are not fulfilled by using their gifts will seek fulfillment in other ways, and those ways are usually destructive. If they are not destructive, they will at the very least be a distraction from their potential. Not using their gifts is akin to not having gifts at all.

Your potential is waiting to be discovered.

No matter what has happened in life, failure is not permanent unless you decide it is permanent. Failure is not an experience … it is a decision. Even then, you have your God-given gifts inside of you that never go away, no matter how dormant they have been or for how long.

You can always pick them up again and use them, and they will always produce good results for you even if you have fears or doubt. God is with you and you can begin today, little by little, step by step, to possess your desires and hopes, even if you do not feel it can happen, it is always worth the risk.

Chapter 17

Envision Your Future

You must have vision for your future. Proverbs 29:18 says that without vision people perish. The next question would have to be, "Perish into what?"

I think the answer is that you will perish into mediocrity, failure, depression, frustration, confusion, minimizing your potential in life, and being unfulfilled. This is why you must dream and take time to write your vision down so that you can know and clarify your own vision.

Designing your vision for the future requires that you allow yourself to dream about where you desire to be in the future. This is called "vision." Your vision for your future is necessary in order to accomplish dreams and goals that you establish to produce results.

Vision is not just wishful thinking or talking a good talk. Some people talk a lot about the future and about what they are going to do, but never create a plan and carry it out. Proverbs says that a lazy man will have thorns (no fruit) in his field and his poverty will come quickly. You can dream your way into laziness and poverty just like the person who never dreams.

No excuses

The difference is carrying out the dream with goals until you get results. Results are the only accurate measuring tool for success. Otherwise you are only a dreamer and a talker which make you sound good at the time, until it becomes apparent that you are just a "talker." Many people have big dreams and their dreams are well thought out. They even design plans to carry out their dreams and visions.

But when it comes time to take action, they self-induce failure by choosing to not cross the "action barrier." You cannot cross the finish line if you do not get in the race and you miss 100% of the shots you do not take! Therefore you must not only have vision and plan it, but you must take action.

There are countless excuses used by the best and smartest people. Perhaps you've heard these excuses before:

- "Let's see what will happen …"
- "I was given a bad hand …"
- "Let's play it by ear …"
- "I wasn't given a chance …"
- "I was born in the wrong family …"

These kinds of statements are excuses, procrastinations, and victim mentalities. The fact is that there will always be obstacles when you plan and take action. You will never do it perfectly, but you must take action and modify if necessary as you go. Take baby steps and cross the action barrier.

There are many people with fewer gifts and talents than you who have accomplished great things! They did so not because they were the best, but because they made themselves disciplined and didn't stop until they had achieved their passions. Remember, failure is not an experience, it is an attitude.

When you maximize your gifts, you can also reach people spiritually for God, and you should do so because that is a part of using your purpose. Your purpose in life is not just to stand in the winner's circle, but to impact other people with God's love. Love never fails.

WHAT'S NEXT?

I challenge you to ask yourself where you desire to be in the next six months and in the next five years. The fact is that you will be doing something and will be somewhere, but if you do not plan it, most likely you will waste time and not make the best of your opportunities. Having vision for your future will help you map out your future based upon your gifts and talents so that you give yourself every opportunity to achieve the desires of your heart.

In order to do this it requires vision and planning. Otherwise you will walk blindly into the future and one day will be unfulfilled with a lack of purpose. Imagine knowing that you did not maximize your God-given potential in your lifetime! And if it is too late to do much about it, wouldn't that be a very disturbing feeling? The good news is that you can do something about it and you can start right now.

You were meant to maximize your gifts!

In order to organize your long-term vision, you can put together some six-month goals that are stepping stones to your five-year vision. Take some time to think about your giftings and write down some ideas about where you want to be in that time frame.

At first, do not spend time thinking about "how" you will carry out the vision and do not jump ahead of yourself by wondering how you can afford it, who will help you, and what to do next. The very first thing you must design in your mind's eye is the "what" of the vision. What is your vision? What do you want to be doing? Answer that question by writing several answers down on paper.

Start now and write your answers down over the next few days. You don't have to be really accurate at first. Just try to tap into your inner desires and identity them. As you write them down, they will become clearer. Your inner heart's desires are somewhere inside of you, even if you think you do not know what they are. Give yourself permission to tap into them and write them down, even if you think they are ridiculous and even if you don't know how you could ever do it.

Do not allow yourself to say, "I don't know." When you say that, those words tell your brain to stop looking. Just keep asking yourself the same question out loud and then dream the answer from inside of you. Then write down whatever comes up inside you, even if it does not make sense.

CREATING A VISION SCENARIO

A good way to create a vision scenario in your mind is to ask yourself: "If I knew I couldn't fail and I had all the resources, what would fulfill me the most, and if I was not afraid, what would I do in the next six months and five years?"

Your answers can be general, specific, or somewhere in between, but write them down. Planning for your future is vital. If you do not plan, you won't arrive because you won't know where you are going. You will arrive at some destination if you get in your car and drive until you run out of gas or get lost. However, you would have not made the best of your time in the way that maximizes your God-given potential in your life. Being active and busy, going anywhere all of your life, will result in some adventure and fun, but will not produce long-lasting results that complete your life purpose.

Ask the questions to yourself and allow thoughts to come up inside of you with no controls, no fears, and no limitations. Do not answer these questions through the eyes or filters of insecurities, inferiorities, or inadequacies that speak to you and cloud your spiritual vision.

Now create your vision scenario by answering the question of your heart's desire in each of the following seven categories:

1. **Spiritual:** spiritual relationship with God, self, and others and how you will fulfill your spiritual purpose

2. **Mental:** education, training, personal development

3. **Emotional:** emotional stability and self-inventory and awareness

4. **Physical:** physical health and bodily condition and appearance

5. **Relational:** relationships include your friends, family, spouse, acquaintances and those with whom you socialize.

6. **Professional:** industry, career pathway, job description, and work ethic (how would I work)

7. **Economical:** income and management

Then look at your answers and ask yourself if those answers match up to your personality strengths, personal gifts, and desires. Now try to think in terms of concept, which is first a broader idea, such as in terms of industries, space, science, math, psychology, imaging, arts, medicine, etc. Then you match up your gifts summary to the industry, and then get specific with where in that industry you match up to maximize your gifts, and then you can be detailed about the specific job description.

For example, let's say you choose medicine, then the type of medicine, then in what setting (hospital, private practice, missionary, etc.), then exactly where and even in what city you would base, and then if you would administrate other doctors and nurses or if you would perform the treatments and have others assist you, and so on.

Once you have answers in all seven categories, then you can write down the "how" for each category. How will you carry out each desire? Create goals that are brief explanations of what it will require to accomplish the vision. Remember, you don't have to be perfect the first time around. Just write down your desires to the best of your ability.

Remember, when you come up with at least one answer in all seven categories, and match them up with the strengths and gifts that you are aware of, the answer that mostly matches up with your gifts and strengths is the dream, industry, or profession you should consider.

If you are in high school or early years in college, you should also choose a college based upon the development and pursuit of your dreams and vision that is in alignment with your personal giftings and personality strengths. Do not attend a college because your friends or boyfriend/girlfriend attend there. This type of fruitless pursuit will preoccupy you and eventually create major regrets in your life.

> **Have you matched your giftings with your desired future?**

You will look back and forever know that you could have done more and been more but gave it up for an emotional time of your life that soon passed. Make decisions based on your personal development. (And if someone is the right one for you, he/she will wait for you and empower you to reach your potential. The exception to this advice is for those whose potential requires that they do it with God's designed person.)

WHAT NEXT?

Once you have completed your answers in all seven categories, then you have begun the process establishing your personal vision for your future! You must realize that God has placed inside of you a desire that will fulfill you the most and will please Him the most! Allow yourself to tap into that dream and write it down. It will also help to pray before or during your time of dreaming this out and answering the questions. When you pray, you are praying from your spirit, which is where your heart's desires are located. They are located there because God put them there. He put them in your heart. That is why they are called the "desires of your heart."

Psalms 34:7 tells us to delight ourselves in the Lord and He will give us the desires of our heart. Why would God want you to know about those desires? I think the reason is to bless you and to bless others as well. Knowing your desires and utilizing them will bless you and also bless others.

The desires of your heart will always involve the use of your God-given gifts. This is true because your gifts always work for you, always fulfill you, and always bless others as well. That is the way God created the system to work.

A client asked me one day what I thought the best system would be for the world, to make it into a better place. My answer was, "Love your neighbor as yourself." Loving people will always involve the use of your gifts. It fulfills you and blesses others.

A REAL EXAMPLE

One client sent me the following true story:

> When I was 15 years old, not yet driving, I went out on a date though I was not allowed. That evening was my first experience with alcohol and I got drunk and passed out in the back seat of my boyfriend's car. When I awoke, my boyfriend was on top of me. I was discombobulated and not aware of what was happening to me. I was still drunk and not sure what to do, so I did nothing. He finished and then took me home. I immediately got into the shower to try to wash off what had just happened. I wasn't sure what to call it back then but now I know it was date rape.
>
> As my life progressed, I began to hate being hot and especially disliked sweating. I got to the point where wearing anything but a sandal made me feel claustrophobic and very uncomfortable. I chalked it up to my weight gain and hormones, but God revealed something very different to me one Tuesday afternoon in Dr. Jones's office.
>
> Dr. Jones had asked me during our last session to meditate on and write down my six-month goal plan and I had prepared accordingly. However when I came into his office, he looked at me and said, "Today we are going to talk about why you don't like to sweat."
>
> I laughed, of course, wondering what this had to do with my personal growth and healing process. To be honest, I never really thought much about it. I didn't like to sweat…so what? But today, God, via Dr. Jones, was going to reveal to me that that was not His plan for my life, and He was going to show me why and break the bonds that held power over my life in this area.

So, Dr. Jones looks at me and asks again, "Without thinking about the answer too much, tell me why you don't like to sweat."

I gave my stock answer which was, "I don't know." He reminded me that that wasn't a viable answer, and as he pressed me to open up my mind and let the Holy Spirit reveal the truth to me, the details of that night came rushing into my mind. It was summer in Texas and very hot, and I was sweating and trapped. I felt what was happening was out of my control and I wasn't sure how to stop it.

I looked up at Dr. Jones and saw instantly the connection, and as I spoke out the details of that night, we began to pray a prayer of release and healing. He told me that not only was this the reason that I did not like heat or sweating, but also why I did not like my feet bound and I saw that this was true. That morning, God set me free from the ties that were binding me that I had not known existed until 15 minutes before my liberation from them was complete. God is so good like that.

That wasn't the only healing. The subject of my daughter is a tender one for me. She is literally the catalyst for all of my maturing, change, and healing. She completed me when she was born. She was a message to me from God of forgiveness, grace, and mercy. When I truly look at her, I see God's love for me. She is in college now, working towards becoming a medical missionary and feels called to the country of Uganda. I am so proud of the woman she is becoming, but we struggled for many years. I spent much of that time believing that she was the problem. I have to say that I was a bit surprised when God revealed that I was the problem and that my past was wreaking havoc on her present life and quite possibly her future. I was especially surprised to find that the root was an area of my life in which I had already experienced healing.

I made the decision to have my first abortion just before my eighteenth birthday. A second followed the next year and yet another pregnancy the following year. What can I say? I give new meaning to the words "fertile Myrtle." I can remember lying on my back in that doctor's office and knowing that I was making the decision to separate myself just a little from God but justifying my behavior due to my youth and volatility of my relationship with the father. The same reasons were used the second time, but by the third, I knew that one more meant that I was not only choosing hell but also insanity. I rededicated my life to the Lord on Easter Sunday 1991 and understood, as I stood in that pew, that by doing so I was choosing to be a mother. I have never once regretted that decision. My daughter brought order to what had been chaos and replaced sorrow and pain with joy and love.

When she was three years old, we were driving home after work and we were stopped at a stop sign in our neighborhood. I turned to look at her and tears filled her eyes and she said to me, "Mommy, do you remember those first two times that you did not have me?"

I said, "Yes," shocked at the words coming from her mouth.

Then she continued, "Jesus and I want you to know that we forgive you and we are just so happy that we are a family again."

I began to cry. I drove home as quickly as possible. Then I really broke down. Had God just really forgiven me through the mouth of my own child for what I considered to me my greatest sin? I spoke to my parents and my pastor, all three of whom were just as flabbergasted as I was. I remember clearly the words of my pastor on the phone that day, "She was meant for you. God was bringing her into your life one way or another." That night was the first time God ministered healing for my abortions into my life.

So, flash forward to my counseling sessions with Dr. Jones and my struggles within my relationship with my daughter. I was enlightened when it was revealed to me that my fears of my daughter repeating my mistakes was the root of our conflict and once released from that fear, we were whole once again. Without Dr. Jones's guidance, I would have believed that I had overcome all the areas of my life once touched by my choice to have an abortion.

It's up to You

Remember, if you do not plant seed you will never produce fruit. I encourage you to water and develop God's gifts that are within you. It's God's seed in you, so plant it. Then produce fruit with those gifts, and by using those gifts, you will, in turn, plant seed into the lives of other people. Furthermore, because the gifts originally come from God, they will always work and will never come up short. They will always be sufficient for every use. But you will always be deficient if you do not operate in your God-given gifts and talents. This may explain why you have not been doing well and how you can begin to prosper.

> **You can do it ... I know you can!**

It is your responsibility to utilize your God-given gifts, strengths, and talents. Worrying and agonizing about it won't help you, but it will distract you. You can regret and agonize where you are in life, or you can use your energy to change it. Write down your vision, create a plan, execute the plan, modify as you go (if necessary), and stay your course until you have your desired results.

Summary

A Few Last Words

Every part of your spirit, mind, emotions, and body is a learning system. God created you to learn what you embrace, believe, and practice. This is a law of behavior that governs all behavior. This law works whether the behavior is productive or destructive, positive, negative, good, or bad. You are not the exception to this law. You cannot practice destructive thinking and behavior and experience a productive outcome. You can only experience a productive, positive outcome if your thinking and actions are productive and positive.

This does not mean you have to be perfect because you won't ever be perfect. It does mean that you program thoughts, and practice the behavior of those thoughts, until they become automatic. It is a law and it will work for you. It is not a respecter of persons. If you work this law, it will work for you. It will work just like a seed planted in soil and watered will produce corresponding fruit. The seed and soil do not care who did the planting. It just processes the seed and produces the fruit. This is exciting because it means that regardless of your negative or positive past, new fruit (results) can be produced!

Learned behavior is developed because of thoughts, beliefs, and behaviors that are practiced over a prolonged period of time that become habit and eventually automatic behavior. It is a conditioning process. This process occurs whether the behavior is productive, destructive, positive, or negative. Behavior moves into the beginning stages of a habit after about 30 days of practice and becomes automatic after about six months of practice.

Automatic behavior is a behavior that is downloaded from the conscious to the subconscious to the unconscious mind and is defined as something that you think, say, or do without conscious, premeditated thought at the time of the behavior. Habit is a behavior that functions on the subconscious level and is a "pattern" but is not yet automatic. A pattern is a series of recurring thoughts or behaviors that forms a certain recurring way of thinking or doing, typically with the same end-results.

The following sequence explains the cycle of learned behavior: Thoughts > Beliefs > Actions > Emotions > Habit > Character (automatic behavior). Prolonged thoughts produce beliefs, emotions, and eventually behavior.

I have broken down the different aspects of behavior and defined them so that you can understand and apply them to your life:

Thoughts:

Mental activity that is practiced as a body of ideas, memories, processing, decisions, imaginations, personality, perceptions, self-image, self-worth, conscience, desires, learning, and associated with certain times in history (past), the present (real time) or the future.

Beliefs:

A belief is any information that is received into the mind or heart and established as truth.

Actions:

Action is an act or response. It constitutes behavior that is acted outwardly (physical activity and motion) or internally (thought activity and emotions). A person can act on a behavior whether that behavior is obvious and overt or unobvious and covert. Spoken words, body posture, smiles, eye motion, eye contact, sounds (sighs), are all included in action.

Emotions:

Emotions include all mental or bodily senses, bodily energy, feelings, excitement, sensations and expressions. A feeling is often defined as an emotion as well. However, feelings are usually identified as related to the body and emotions usually are related to the central nervous system expressions. Energy generates through the central nervous system and is felt inside the body, and is accompanied by internal thought messages and impulses, like passion, anger, hurt, fear, rejection, etc. Emotions can also be remembered in the body (muscle memory) and central nervous system (emotional memory).

Habit:

A pattern of behavior just below the surface (past tense) minimum of 30 days of practice and encoding...the beginning of the neurological pathway construction.

Automatic Behavior:

Automatic behavior is also called character. Behavior can be so automatic that it becomes a person's character. Automatic behavior is also unconscious behavior and requires a minimum of six months practice before it becomes automatic. Automatic behavior is encoded into the unconscious mind and is defined as something you think, say, or do without conscious, premeditated intent at the time of the behavior. This stage of behavior development or change is the final stages of the neurological pathway construction.

This means that when a behavior is practiced, neurological pathways are constructed because you are practicing. The neurological pathways are like highways that accommodate traffic. The pathways accommodate the firing and flow of neurotransmitters that are fired by neurons full of energy. As the neurons fire, they create pathways that are connected by synapses that bind together the sections of the highway. These highways accommodate the behavior that you are practicing. You can remember it this way: what fires, wires. Your most frequently acted out behavior begins to wire and eventually becomes automatic behavior that flows naturally without making you act it out.

The Human System:

God created us as complex living beings. We are made up of a system that is spirit, mind, emotions, and body. This is a system because all four of these parts work together synergistically to function as one whole. If all of the parts of the system are healthy then the entire system can work together in wholeness. Health is each individual part functioning in their designed purpose. Wholeness means that all the healthy separate parts work together as a whole or entire networking system.

Unhealthy parts require that other parts of the system overcompensate and suffer for the deficiencies and unhealthiness in them. An unhealthy mind will negatively affect the body through physical destructiveness, abuse or neglect to the body. An unhealthy or dead spirit will affect the mind, emotions, and body by carrying the burdens of past wounds, hurts and pain, alone, without allowing God's help. Unhealthy emotions will impulsively escalate a person into an offense to lash out without being able to intervene or prevent the escalation. Unhealthy emotions also create unpredictability, moods, and hypersensitivities. Unhealthy emotions also create self-medicating with comfort food, overspending, alcohol, drug abuse and more.

I describe our human system (which is commonly described as spirit, soul, and body) as a Divinely molded and bound together union of four parts, which include:

> **1. The spirit:** Also called the heart, this is the "real" us. The original created part of God that was breathed into man's physical body which will always remain in existence even after the body dies. The spirit can be fed, unfed, nurtured, not nurtured, clean, dirty, righteous, evil, cultivated, uncultivated, soft, hard, ruled, unruly, a habitation, alive, dead, light, dark, willing, unwilling, stirred,

unstirred, serving, not serving, repentant, unrepentant, proud, humble, desirous, not desirous and is always eternal.

2. **The mind:** A part of the soul with direction of thinking, the mind includes all thought activity and is also called the psyche, from which we get the word psychology. The mind is made of what I call "arenas" of the mind which I dissect into the following categories: Intellect (processing, decisions, reasoning), learning (acquire, get knowledge, understand), memory (reference points from learning, accept, store and recall information), personality (behavioral characteristics or strengths and weaknesses which identify a person's uniqueness), desires (wish, long for, crave, covet, strong appetite), conscience (discern the difference between right and wrong, moral sense or judgment, ethics) and beliefs (information received and accepted as truth).

3. **The emotions:** A part of the soul with feelings and sensations initiated by thoughts and generated from and through the central nervous system, and also stored as memory in the brain (emotional memory), body (muscle memory), bodily organs, and the central nervous system (encoded as a behavior).

4. **The body:** The whole physical substance of a human being, physical mass or body or group, a tangible object, flesh, bones, organs, physical motion, physical expressions and experiences, physical existence, physical evidence, bodily material substance.

The reason it is important to describe our system, is to state that this entire human system can learn, memorize and express itself synergistically, based upon its health and programming. If each part of this entire system is healthy and is working together as created, then the person is a "whole" person. This type of condition does not happen accidentally or just because more time passes by. Rather, it happens because a person decides to be healthy and whole, at the risk of failure. It takes work, and cannot be achieved alone. Everyone needs help and everyone needs God. There are no exceptions.

Pursue the knowledge you need to improve your life. The Holy Scriptures state, you shall know the truth and the truth shall make you free. It is not the knowledge alone that makes you free, but having knowledge of the truth that makes you free. Of course the basic source of all knowledge is the inspired Word of God.

When you gain knowledge and embrace it, you experience freedom from the distractions that have been in opposition to that knowledge. Remember, you can't possibly know everything about every topic. This is especially true in areas of your life where you find yourself continuously struggling.

Behavior is not accidental: behavior patterns are developed when a belief is practiced over time. Gradually the behavior becomes a habit, and eventually a part of your character.

In what area of life do you struggle the most? These struggles represent your weaknesses; where you have a lack of knowledge. You must gain more knowledge in this area and develop your strengths instead of trying to operate in your weaknesses. Look for people and organizations with whom to align yourself, who have had success in your weaknesses and learn from them. You cannot afford to seek knowledge from unsuccessful and unknowledgeable people. Gain and understand a fresh knowledge, which will replace the old with the new. Then practice this new knowledge with absolute determination, regardless of how you feel.

You must not allow yourself to become "feelings motivated." Feelings are not always relevant or realistic. Success does not ride on the wings of emotional motivation.

As the freedom process is integrated into your system, it will empower you to continue the new behavior you are pursuing. The more positive experiences you have, the more building blocks you will create. This will prove to you that you are empowered to change.

Put simply, it is confidence. If in the transition you experience old feelings of failure or fear of the unknown, remember this; the emotions are real but they are not telling you the truth and therefore they are not valid. Do not embrace emotions just because you feel them. In doing so you are validating them as truth. Knowledge, wisdom, understanding and discretion will tell you the truth. The old emotions are most likely a part of the same recurring struggles and weaknesses. They are a part of your old programming, which must be removed and replaced with new ones.

History shows us many examples of people who were empowered by each other's knowledge and gifts. Remember how Harry Firestone, Alexander Bell and Henry Ford all built houses next to each other? This kind of relationship is proof of how people with knowledge can make a positive impact on each other as well as on the entire world. Each one possessed unique knowledge that was recognized and embraced by the other. Pride or arrogance did not prevent them from learning from each other. They obviously knew something that many people do not know. This lesson is powerful. You can do the same!

We all have 24 hours in a day. No more, no less. God is not a respecter of persons. He gives to all and loves all equally in this way. You have 24 hours in every day to make the choices that will develop your God-given potential. Allow your 24 hours to bring you new experiences and new knowledge. Maximize and pursue this opportunity. Seek and you shall find.

If you can't make the changes you desire alone, get with someone who will encourage and influence you. You are never alone, because God is with you and He will never forsake you. It is time for you to make the choice to change. Do it with desperation and do it now. If not now, when?

Success comes when you are no longer willing to tolerate anything less. Now embrace this knowledge and use it. It will empower you.

I pray God's richest blessings in your life as you fulfill His Divine purpose. Continue to be encouraged.

Dr. Mark Jones, LMFT

If you are ready to resolve your past, restore your health, and retrain your thinking, you must attend my Trinity Program. For more information, see my website and contact my office.

Notes

My Steps to Healing

www.LibertyAllianceGroup.com